General Principles

of

Criminal Law

(Islamic and Western)

Imran Ahsan Khan Nyazee

Center for Excellence in Research
Islamabad

Center for Excellence in Research,
Head Office: No. 103, Street 2, PTV Colony,
Shahpur, Islamabad,
Pakistan 44000

First Published: 1998
Second Edition: 2016

CENTER FOR EXCELLENCE IN RESEARCH

For my son, Ibrahim

TABLE OF CONTENTS

PREFACE 9

I THE NATURE, PURPOSE AND FUNCTION OF CRIMINAL LAW 11

Ch. 1 What is a Crime? 13
1.1 The Significance of the Criminal Law 13
1.2 The Definition of Crime 15
1.2.1 Recognizing a crime as a public wrong . . 16
1.2.2 Recognizing a crime as a moral wrong . . 18
1.2.3 Recognizing crime through criminal proceedings 20
1.3 General Conclusion 22
1.4 The Distinction Between "Offence"and "Crime" 22

Ch. 2 Origins, Structure and Sources of the Criminal Law 25
2.1 Principles Governing Criminal Law in Pakistan 25
2.2 The Structure of the Criminal Law 27
2.2.1 The propositions of criminal law 27
2.2.2 Functional structure of propositions . . . 27
2.2.3 The meaning of principles 29
2.3 The Sources of Criminal Law in Pakistan . . . 29
2.4 The Pakistan Penal Code: The Nature of Legislation on Criminal Law 31
2.4.1 Lord McCauley on the Penal Code 31
2.4.2 Archibald Galloway on Islamic Law Versus Common Law 34

Ch. 3 Criminal Law and the Constitution **39**
3.1 Significant Articles of the Constitution 40
3.1.1 Article on Rule of Law 40
3.1.2 High Treason 41
3.1.3 Laws Against Fundamental Rights Void . 41
3.1.4 Security of Life and Liberty 42
3.1.5 Safeguards as to Arrest and Detention . . 43
3.1.6 Right to Fair Trial and Due Process 43
3.1.7 No Retrospective Punishment 44
3.1.8 Double Jeopardy and Self-Incrimination . 44
3.2 Legality: *Nulla Poena Sine Lege* 45
3.2.1 Brief history of the principle 46
3.2.2 Origins of the principle in Islam 47
3.2.3 Main Implications of the Principle 48
3.2.3.1 The void-for-vagueness rule . . . 49
3.2.3.2 Constitutional limitations on crime creation 49
3.2.3.3 The criminal statutes are to be construed strictly 50
3.2.3.4 Effect of repeal 52

Ch. 4 Classification of Offences **53**
4.1 Classification of Crimes in Western Law . . . 53
4.1.1 Earlier classifications 53
4.1.1.1 Bracton 53
4.1.1.2 Hale 54
4.1.1.3 Blackstone 55
4.1.1.4 East, Russel, and Gabbet 56
4.1.1.5 Bentham, Austin, Stephen and Kenny 56
4.1.1.6 American writers 57
4.2 Classification of Crimes in Islamic Law 57
4.2.1 Classification on the basis of the right affected: *ḥadd, ta'zīr* and *siyāsah* 57
4.2.2 Why the classification into *ḥadd* and *ta'zīr*? 61
4.2.3 Differences between *ta'zīr* and *siyāsah* . . 64
4.3 Modern Classifications in Law 67

Ch. 5 Punishment and Sentencing **69**
5.1 The Aims of Western Criminal Law 69
5.2 The Aims of Islamic Criminal Law 70
5.2.1 The protection of interests 71
5.2.2 Priorities within interests 73
5.3 The Nature of Punishment 73
5.3.1 The purposes of sentencing and the Model Penal Code 73
5.3.2 The essential ingredients of punishment . 74
5.3.3 Analysis of the ingredients of punishment 75
5.3.4 Types of punishments: Western and Islamic 77
5.3.5 Is imprisonment the preferred penalty in Islam? 78

Ch. 6 Theories of Punishment **81**
6.1 The Theory of Retribution 82
6.1.1 Moral blameworthiness 83
6.1.2 Proportionality to guilt 86
6.1.2.1 Desire for vengeance. 89
6.1.2.2 The harm done 90
6.1.2.3 The sentence to fit the crime . . . 91
6.1.2.4 Justice and equality 91
6.2 Deterrence or the Protection of the Public . . 92
6.2.1 Primary and secondary deterrence 92
6.2.2 Deterrence and Islamic law 95
6.3 The Theory of Reformation and Rehabilitation 97
6.4 The Theory of Prevention 98
6.5 General Conclusion: Integrative Approach . . 99

II GENERAL PRINCIPLES OF CRIMINAL LAW **101**

Ch. 7 Elements of Crime, Criminal Process and Burden of Proof **103**
7.1 Adversarial and Inquisitorial Processes 103
7.1.1 Responsibility for marshalling evidence for trial 104

7.1.2 Relative faith in the integrity of pre-trial processes 105
7.1.3 The extent of discretion 105
7.1.4 The nature of the trial process 106
7.1.5 The role of the victim 106
7.2 Criminal Process 107
7.2.1 Investigation 108
7.2.2 Prosecution 110
7.2.3 Trial 110
7.3 Criminal Liability and Elements of a Crime . 111
7.4 The Nature of the Elements 112
7.5 Burden of Proof 113

Ch. 8 *Actus Reus* and Causation 115
8.1 Physical Act: *Actus Reus* 115
8.1.1 The meaning of *actus reus* 115
8.1.2 Rules for the *actus reus* 117
8.1.2.1 The *actus reus* must be proved . . 117
8.1.2.2 The Act Must Be Voluntary . . . 119
8.1.2.3 Causation: The act should be causative 121
8.1.3 A "State of Affairs" as an *actus reus* 122
8.1.4 Omission as an "Act" 122
8.1.5 Possession as an "Act" 123

Ch. 9 *Mens Rea* 125
9.1 Mental State (*Mens Rea*) 125
9.1.1 The meaning of *mens rea* 125
9.1.1.1 Intention 126
9.1.1.2 Recklessness 130
9.1.1.3 Negligence 131
9.1.2 Basic *mens rea* 131
9.2 Concurrence of *Mens Rea* With the *Actus Reus* 132
9.3 Islamic Law and *Mens Rea* (*'Amd*) 133
9.3.1 *'Amd* and its External Standards 133
9.3.2 External standards and the law of *qiṣāṣ* . . 135
9.4 Negligence and *Mens Rea* 136

9.4.1 Negligence as non-compliance with an objective standard 136
9.4.2 Negligence and Islamic law 138
9.4.2.1 Should negligence be a basis for liability 138

Ch. 10 Strict Liability Offences 141
10.1 The meaning of strict liability 142
10.2 Strict liability at common law 142
10.3 Examples of strict liability offences in Pakistan 143
10.4 Recognition of strict liability offences 143
10.5 Why is strict liability imposed? 144
10.6 Strict liability and Islamic law 145

Ch. 11 Parties to Crimes and Inchoate Offences 147
11.1 Accomplice Liability at Common Law 147
11.2 Understanding Important Concepts 148
11.3 Criminal Conspiracy 151
11.3.1 Meaning of Criminal Conspiracy 151
11.3.2 Object of Criminal Conspiracy: Illegal Act 151
11.3.3 Essential Ingredients of Criminal Conspiracy 152
11.3.4 Punishment for Criminal Conspiracy . . . 153
11.4 Abetment of an Offence 153
11.5 Who is an Abettor? 155
11.6 Inchoate Offences 156
11.6.1 The Meaning of Inchoate Offences 156
11.6.2 Attempt 157
11.6.3 Islamic law, Abetment, and Attempt . . . 158

Ch. 12 Capacity 161
12.1 Infancy 161
12.1.1 Presumptions at common law 161
12.1.2 Pakistan and common law countries . . . 162
12.1.3 Infancy and Islamic law 162
12.1.3.1 As applied in Pakistan 163
12.1.3.2 As it exists in traditional law . . . 164
12.2 Insanity 166

12.2.1 The governing provision and rules 166
12.2.2 Mental condition during criminal proceedings 170
12.3 Vicarious Liability Offences 171
12.3.1 Limitation on punishment 171
12.3.2 Implying vicarious liability from a strict liability offence 172
12.3.3 Liability of corporations and associations 172
12.3.4 Corporate Manslaughter 173

Ch. 13 General Defences **175**
13.1 Necessity—Pressure from Physical or Natural Forces 175
13.1.1 Necessity and Islamic law 176
13.2 Duress (Compulsion or Coercion)—A Human Threat 176
13.2.1 Coercion and duress (*ikrāh*) in Islamic law 177
13.2.1.1 Traditional Islamic law 177
13.2.1.2 As applied in Pakistan 179
13.3 Mistake 179
13.3.1 Mistake or Ignorance of fact 179
13.3.2 Mistake or Ignorance of Law 181
13.3.3 Mistake in Islamic law—*jahl, shubhāt* . . . 181
13.4 Consent 184
13.4.1 Euthanasia and Islamic law 185
13.5 The Right of Private Defence 185
13.5.1 How is the right exercised 186
13.5.2 Private-defence and Islamic law 187

Ch. 14 Mental Capacity Defences **189**
14.1 Insanity as a Mental Capacity Defence 189
14.2 Automatism as a Mental Capacity Defence . . 189
14.3 Intoxication 189
14.3.1 Voluntary intoxication 190
14.3.2 Involuntary intoxication 191
14.3.3 Intoxication and Islamic law 192

Ch. 15 Overview of Offences and Penalties in Islamic Law 195

15.1 *Ḥadd* Penalties 195
15.1.1 *Zinā* or unlawful sexual intercourse . . . 196
15.1.2 *Qadhf* or false accusation of unlawful sexual intercourse 197
15.1.3 *Shurb* or drinking of wine or intoxicating beverages 197
15.1.4 *Sariqah* or theft 198
15.1.5 *Ḥirābah* or Highway Robbery 199
15.1.6 Apostasy (*Riddah*) 199
15.2 *Jināyat* (Bodily Injuries) and *Qiṣāṣ* 200
15.2.1 *Qatl 'Amd* or Murder 200
15.2.2 *Shibh al-'amd* or culpable homicide not amounting to murder 201
15.2.3 *Qatl khaṭa'* or manslaughter 201
15.2.4 *Qatl bi-al-sabab* or indirect homicide . . . 202
15.2.5 Justifiable homicide 203
15.2.6 Bodily harm 203
15.3 *Ta'zīr* or penalties imposed by the state 203
15.4 *Siyāsah shar'īyah* or the administration of justice 205
15.5 *Ghaṣb* (Usurpation, Misappropriation) 207
15.6 Destruction of Property (*Itlāf*) 208

Bibliography 209

Index 213

PREFACE

Experience indicates that some people are irritated, or find it difficult to concentrate, when the text stands completely merged during comparison of two legal systems. This book, therefore, adopts a different methodology. Under each main heading in a chapter, it presents the Western point of view first. Once this has been explained, the Islamic point of view on the same issue is stated whenever it is felt necessary or is available. This method will not only assist the reader in understanding better the two points of view, but will also help those who wish to skip either point of view. On certain occasions a complete merger is unavoidable.

It should be noted that this is a preliminary book and it will not be possible to state the position of Islamic law on each point or in such detail that may be expected. This does not mean that there are no views from the perspective of Islamic law on the issue; it means that a fuller comparison can only be undertaken in a more comprehensive study.

For the principles of Western law discussed in this book, reliance has been placed mostly on the excellent and exhaustive book *Criminal Law* by J. C. Smith and Brian Hogan. Some other important works used include works by Jerome Hall, Cross and Jones and Weinreb. Kenny's book written in 1902, though recommended in the syllabus, is outdated and many of his views and formulations have been rejected by modern writers. A select bibliography is provided at the end. As compared to the earlier editions of this book, the structure has been revised as has some of the content.

Imran Ahsan Khan Nyazee
Islamabad
September, 2016

Part I

THE NATURE, PURPOSE AND FUNCTION OF CRIMINAL LAW

CHAPTER 1

WHAT IS A CRIME?

The more corrupt the republic, the more numerous the laws.

Tacitus, *Annals*

1.1 The Significance of the Criminal Law

Every society, says Scheb, faces the fundamental problem of achieving social control—"protecting people's lives and property and establishing socially desirable levels of order, harmony, safety, and decency."[1] Social control through criminal law works hand in hand with other informal methods of such control includ-

1. John M. Scheb and John M. Scheb II, *Criminal Law and Procedure*, 7th ed. (Belmont, CA: Wadsworth, Cengage Learning, 2011), 3. Here is what Kenny, a famous criminal law writer, said: "For this branch of study is rendered attractive to all thoughtful men by its direct bearing on the most urgent social difficulties of our time and on the deepest ethical problems of all times. And almost all men, whether thoughtful or thoughtless, are fascinated by its dramatic character—the vivid and violent nature of the events which criminal courts notice and repress, as well as of those by which they effect the repression. Forcible interferences with property and liberty, with person and life, are the causes which bring criminal law into operation; and its operations are themselves directed to the infliction of similar acts of seizure, suffering, and slaughter. The utmost violence which administrators of civil justice have power to inflict ranks only among the gentlest of those penalties by which the criminal courts do their work. Hence of all branches of legal study there is no other which stirs men's imaginations and sympathies so readily and so deeply." Courtney Stanhope Kenny, *Outlines of Criminal Law*, 2nd ed. (New York, NY: The Macmillan Company, 1907), 1.

ing family structures, social norms, and religious precepts.[2] Criminal law directly prohibits conduct, and is the subject of heated debate.[3] The first thing that comes to the mind of the citizen when he thinks of the law are visions of crimes being committed, of handcuffs, of police, and of prosecution in court. The same feeling is reflected in the media as well, and most of the interesting news are those that are related to the criminal law. All this reflects the importance society attaches to this branch of the law and the awe that this law sometimes inspires.

Most societies agree upon the types of conduct that should be prohibited. Thus, murder, robbery, theft, and damage to propety are considered injurious in most societies. In certain societies, however, some types of conduct are considered criminal at times, but are not at other times. Thus, in some Western societies homosexuality was once a crime, but today it is not. Today, it may be a crime for a man to rape his wife, but in earlier times is was not. "As general attitudes change over time, so do attitudes to the kinds of behaviour we label as criminal."[4] This may not be the case in Muslim societies, like Pakistan, where much of the criminal law is still coloured by ideas arising from religion.[5] In such societies, many of the traditional types of crimes are likely to remain stable.

It may be expected that in a criminal law system influenced by religion, as in a country like Pakistan, there may be clarity in declaring certain types of conduct as criminal, but in practice this may not be so. Thus, there may be confusion whether prohibited acts that give rise to blood-money (*diyat*) are really torts or crimes. The confusion has always existed in the criminal law. It has not been clear as to what types of conduct is to be deemed criminal. The lack of clarity usually makes it difficult to justify the penal-

2. Scheb and II, *Criminal Law and Procedure*, 3.
3. Catherine Elliott and Frances Quinn, *Criminal Law*, 8th ed. (Essex: Pearson Education Limited, 2010), 2.
4. Ibid., 2.
5. Today, the law of crimes in Pakistan includes the *ḥudūd*, *qiṣāṣ*, *diyat* and blasphemy laws. It is possible that in the near future there may be other types of conduct that may be declared criminal on the basis of Islamic law.

ties associated with the commission of the prohibited acts. This leads to the haphazard enhancements of penalties, just as it leads to overcriminaliztion.[6] In this chapter, we will deal mainly with the criteria on the basis of which we declare acts as crimes. In other words, we will attempt to answer the question: what is a crime?

1.2 The Definition of Crime

The definition of crime should enable us to look at an act (or omission) and say that this is a crime, but in practice, in the criminal law, it is almost impossible to do so.[7] It is for this reason that def-

6. Anyone who surveys the reform activity of the Law and Justice Commission in this area in the last few decades, or reviews the changes proposed in the criminal law by the Ministry of Law and Justice, will definitely get this feeling.
7. "When a student of criminal law is asked to define the subject matter of his field of study, he is immediately put into a position somewhat reminiscent of a First World War infantryman being sent over the top to negotiate his way through a minefield of unexpected procedural, linguistic and philosophic difficulties. The main problem originates from the fact that the concept of crime encompasses two distinct although overlapping ideas: that of behaviour; and that of the official status, or criminal label, which is attached to the behaviour. Because the official status of the same behaviour may well change over time, it is impossible to formulate a definition which would enable us to identify any individual act as a crime or not a crime.When the criminal label is applied to, or removed from, a particular form of behaviour by the legislature or the courts, the nature of the act does not change only its legal status. Any attempt at a definition of crime based on behaviour will include a description of the behaviour both when it is and when it is not afforded the status of a crime. For example, the act of taking one's own life was a crime until the Suicide Act 1961 made this activity perfectly lawful. The nature and, possibly, the morality of the act of suicide did not change dramatically in 1961, but its legal status did." Roger Geary, *Understanding Criminal Law* (London: Cavendish Publishing Limited, 2002), 1. Compare this with the law of suicide in the Pakistan Penal Code and then reflect upon what Islamic law has to say about it, especially in the context of terrorism.

initions have become unfashionable in the law these days. What writers normally do is to describe the characteristics of a crime.[8] This description enables them to identify acts as crimes. The description of these characteristics, therefore, follows:

1.2.1 Recognizing a crime as a public wrong

Law: A crime consists of an act that has a particularly harmful effect on the public and does more than merely interfere with private rights. In modern law, the state is the defender of the rights of the public.

The public nature of a crime is evidenced by the contrast between the rules of civil and criminal procedure. Thus, subject to certain provisions, any citizen can initiate a criminal prosecution whether or not he has suffered a special harm over and above other members of the public. In practice, of course, a vast majority of prosecutions are carried on by the police or other public officers who have no personal interest in the outcome.[9] Further, the individual who starts a prosecution may not discontinue it at will for it is not only his concern but that of every citizen. In addition, the initiater of the prosecution has no power to pardon the offender. This right belongs to the state, which represents the public interest in the matter.[10]

In the law, however, this contrasts sharply with civil wrongs—torts and breaches of contract. In civil wrongs, only the person injured may sue. He (and only he) may freely discontinue the proceedings at any time and, if he succeeds and an award of damages is made in his favour, he may, at his entire discretion forgive the defendant and terminate his liability.

Islamic law: In Islamic law, on the other hand, there are a number of rights that may be affected by a criminal act. These are

8. J. C. Smith and Brian Hogan, *Criminal Law*, 2nd ed. (London: Butterworths, 1983), 3; David Omerod, *Criminal Law: Smith & Hogan*, 11th ed. (Oxford: Oxford University Press, 2005), 9.
9. Smith and Hogan, *Criminal Law*, 18. This statement may not be true for a society in which corruption is rampant.
10. Under §345 of the Cr.P.C., some offences are compoundable with the permission of the court and some without such permission.

the rights of Allah as in most *ḥudūd*, the rights of Allah mixed up with the rights of individuals as in *qiṣāṣ* and *qadhf*, and rights involved in *ta'zīr* and *siyāsah* offences. Ḥanafī jurists maintain that *ta'zīr* offences affect the rights of individuals, but this may mean the rights of individuals collectively, which is what we mean by public rights. *Siyāsah* offences are considered to affect the right of the *imām* or the state and these again are public rights. In modern times the distinction between *ta'zīr* and *siyāsah* offences has been ignored, and both are referred to as *ta'zīr* offences.[11] On the whole, we may assume that a crime, in Islamic law too, affects public rights. Even when the right is purely the right of Allah, as in *ḥudūd*, the responsibility rests on the state, because the *state owes the right to Allah to implement the ḥudūd*.[12]

In Islamic law, the position is the same with respect to the intiation of criminal proceedings, but in the case of *qiṣāṣ* the aggrieved person, ususally the heir, has the right to pardon the offender through the procedure laid down for *sulḥ* in accordance with Ḥanafī law.[13] Even in *qiṣāṣ*, under certain circumstances, the state still retains the right to punish habitual offenders who have been pardoned by the heirs of the victim. On the whole, the characteristics of offences pertaining to life and bodily injuries are akin to torts. This may be the reason why such offences are classified as *jināyāt* by the Ḥanafī jurists. As already indicated, the term *jināyah* is applied by Ḥanafī jurists to mean homicide and bodily injuries as well as to torts. Al-Sarakhsī says:

11. It is extremely important to understand how the earlier jurists classified crimes, even if this classification has been altered somewhat in modern times for reasons of expediency or for lack of complete understanding of the structure of this law. We shall study this classification in chapter 5, and note the changes made in modern times. For a distinction between *ta'zīr* and *siyāsah* .
12. The detailed discussion about the various kinds of rights and crimes associated with them will be undertaken in chapter 4, which deals with the classification of crimes.
13. The Qisas and Diyat provisions of the Penal Code and the Cr.P.C. provide in *sulḥ* that the agrieved person will pardon the offender with the permission of the trial judge. Thus, here too the state is involved and retains some right.

> Know that the term *jināyah* (جناية) (crime) is used for an act that is forbidden by the law irrespective of its being directed at property or life, but in the jargon of the *fuqahā'* the term *jināyah* is applied to an act directed against life and limbs. They designated the act against property by the term *qhaṣb* (غصب) when the general usage is different from it.[14]

The remaining schools apply the term *jināyah* to mean a crime generally. The use of this term, however, does not change the attributes of offences pertaining to homicides and bodily injuries, and they do retain some attributes of civil wrongs.

CRIMES, IN LAW AS WELL AS IN ISLAMIC LAW ON THE WHOLE, are wrongs that are sufficiently injurious to the public to warrant the application of criminal procedure to deal with them. Of course, this does not enable us to recognize an act as a crime when we see one. Some acts are so obviously harmful to the public that anyone would be able to say they should be criminal, but there are many others about which opinions may differ widely.

1.2.2 Recognizing a crime as a moral wrong

Law: The second characteristic of crimes is that they are acts that are morally wrong. Considering a crime a moral wrong is the traditional attitude. Today, the test of immorality is not very helpful, especially in the West, and there has been considerable debate about whether an act ought to be a crime simply on the ground that it is immoral. For example in England, the Wolfendon Committee on Homosexual Offences and Prostitution maintained that:

> It is not…the function of the law to intervene in the private lives of citizens, or to seek to enforce any particular pattern of behaviour further than it is necessary to carry out the purposes we have outlined.[15]

14. Shams al-A'immah Sarakhsī, *Kitāb al-Mabsūṭ*, ed. Abū 'Abd Allāh Ismā'īl al Shāfi'ī, 30 vols. (Beirut: Dār al-Kutub al-'Ilmiyyah, 2001), vol. 27, 84.
15. (1957) Cmnd. 247, para 13 as quoted in Smith and Hogan, *Criminal Law*, 19.

This view was challenged by Lord Devlin, who argued that there is a public morality which is an essential part of the bondage which keeps society together; and that society must use the criminal law to preserve morality in the same way that it uses it to protect and preserve anything else that is essential to its existence.[16] It should not be assumed here that morality is based upon religious beliefs rather it is what society at a certain time considers good or bad, right or wrong. This is meant when it is said that the standard of morality is that of "the man in the jury box."[17]

In the West, there are those who maintain that it is not proper for the state to enforce the general morality without asking whether it is based upon ignorance, superstition or misunderstanding. But, others ask, if we are not to base criminal law on the general morality, does this imply that "our law making is or should be controlled by independent gods of Pure Reason, installed somewhere in our political systems and endowed with power to determine such questions for society, free of the prejudices to which lesser men are subject?"

In England, the House of Lords has repudiated the suggestion that it has power to extend the criminal law to enforce good morals. The Sexual Offences Act 1967 made homosexuality between consenting adults legal. The enforcement of morality, as such, by the criminal law is losing ground in the West.[18]

Islamic law: In Islamic law, crimes are generally associated with sin (*ma'siyah*). Thus, crimes have to be morally wrong. Further, this morality is not based upon what the public may consider to be right or wrong, that is, moral or immoral, rather it is the Lawgiver who determines the morality or immorality of an act. Islamic law would uphold the statement of Lord Devlin that society should use the criminal law to preserve morality in the same way that it uses it to preserve and protect anything that is essential to its existence. The enforcement of morals is a requirement that flows

16. Ibid.
17. Ibid.
18. Ibid., 20. In England, the age for consenting to homosexuality has recently been lowered to sixteen years.

directly out of the purposes of Islamic law, as we shall see in the next chapter.

Enforcement of morality based on religious norms is the primary duty of an Islamic state. Yet, there are those in Muslim countries who would maintain the other view, and voices can be heard in Muslim countries calling for a separation between religion and state, that is, the state should not be entrusted the task of enforcing the general morality. In Muslim countries, it is up to the people and their elected representatives to decide whether religion and state should go their separate ways, but one thing is certain that if such separation occurs the enforcement of morality, which is a major goal of the Islamic criminal law, will gradually fail.

1.2.3 Recognizing crime through criminal proceedings

Law: Faced with the difficulty in identifying and defining the criminal quality of an act, most writers as well as the courts in the West usually rely upon the the nature of the proceedings that follow the commission of a criminal act. The requirement then is of distinguishing criminal proceedings from civil proceedings. It is the same difficulty that is faced when we try to distinguish between crimes and torts; namely, that most torts are crimes as well, though some torts are not crimes and some crimes are not torts. It is not in the nature of the act, but in the nature of the proceedings that the distinction consists; and generally both types of proceedings may follow where an act is both a crime and a tort.[19]

Several writers, like Kenny and Winfield, tried to define crime in terms of criminal proceedings, however, the definition given by Williams is considered better.[20] He said that a crime is:

> An act that is capable of being followed by criminal proceedings, having one of the types of outcome known to follow these proceedings.[21]

The test that emerges from all this, and which is consistently applied, is whether the proceeding following the commission of

19. Ibid.
20. Ibid.
21. 8 CLP 107 at 123 as quoted in Smith and Hogan, *Criminal Law*, 22.

an act results in the punishment of the offender. This test, it is maintained, appears to work well enough in practice.[22]

But the test is not considered completely satisfactory, and writers point out that it is a rule with exceptions, because some actions for penalties are undoubtedly civil actions, and yet they have the punishment of the offender as their objective. For this reason the test of punishment is jurisprudentially unsatisfactory. In addition to this, those who are not fully satisfied with the test say that the meaning of punishment itself is not easy to ascertain; for example the defendant in a civil case, who is ordered to pay damages by way of compensation, may well feel that he has been punished. These thinkers suggest that the distinction between a criminal and civil sanction turns upon a judgement of community condemnation that accompanies and justifies the imposition of punishment.[23]

According to this view it is the condemnation, plus the consequences of the sentence—fine or imprisonment—which together constitute the punishment; but the condemnation is the essential feature. From this, it is argued that "we can say readily enough what a 'crime' is":

> It is not simply anything which the legislature chooses to call a "crime." It is not simply anti-social conduct which public officers are given a responsibility to suppress. It is not simply any conduct to which a legislature chooses to attach a "criminal" penalty. It is conduct which, if duly shown to have taken place, will incur a formal and solemn pronouncement of the moral condemnation of the community.[24]

It is obvious that "the formal and solemn pronouncement" means the judgement of a criminal court, however, if the matter rests on the judgement of the court, then, we go back to the

22. Ibid.
23. Ibid., 23.
24. H. M. Hart, "The Aims of the Criminal Law" (1958) 23 *Law and Contemporary Problems,* 405 as quoted in Smith and Hogan, *Criminal Law,* 23.

initial question as to whether the proceedings following the commission of an act are civil or criminal. For the courts this guidance comes from the legislature, which prescribes whether the proceeding shall be criminal and whether punitive measures shall be taken.

Islamic law: In Islamic law, we realize the truth of this assertion in the case of homicide and offences against the human body. While many of the characteristics of these acts resemble those of torts and civil wrongs, the proceedings that follow their commission are criminal. It is for this reason that such offences are considered crimes and not torts, yet, the conceptual difficulty remains.

The test of criminal proceedings is applied not only to determine whether an act is a crime or a civil wrong, it is also used to distinguish between different categories of offences. This is explained at some length in the classification of crimes in Islamic law.

1.3 General Conclusion

On the whole, we can say that for Islamic law as well as positive law a crime is an act that violates public rights and is followed up by criminal proceedings and punitive measures. Such an act may be a moral wrong in the postive law, but in Islamic law it usually is. One thing that is obvious is that when we talk of a crime as an act or omission followed by criminal proceedings, we are in reality talking about an offence and not crime in the meaning of felonies or *jināyāt* (See next section).

1.4 The Distinction Between "Offence"and "Crime"

Section 40 of the Penal Code states that "the word 'offence' denotes a thing made punishable by this Code." (Note the word "thing" instead of an "act" or "omission."). Section 4(o) of the Criminal Procedure Code says that "Offence" means "any act or omission made punishable by any law for the time being in force."

The codes talk in terms of "offence" and not crime. Are the two words then synonymous? Does the word "crime" have some other meaning? Is every act or omission that invokes criminal proceedings a crime?

It is not accurate to describe "criminal proceeding" as one for the punishment of crime; for it is also employed for the punishment of some offences not regarded as crimes in the ordinary meaning of the term. Most criminal justice systems developed initially to deal with crimes of violence, and at a later stage for crimes against the security of the state. In more recent times criminal proceedings have been increasingly employed to deal with commercial crimes, and departing still from its original uses, with offences against regulatory laws.[25] The latter acts or omissions are not inherently anti-social and usually do not require a criminal intent.[26]

We may, therefore, say that not all punishable offences are crimes. There is a category of petty offences to which the term crime is not commonly applied, even though the procedure for trying and punishing them resembles that used in connection with crimes. The distinction, however, rests on the severity of punishment prescribed rather than the inherent nature of the offence. The use of the word crime is better understood through the the early classification into felonies, misdemeanours and petty offences. We shall have more to say when we look at the classification of crimes.

In Islamic law too the approach has been somewhat similar though not exactly. The word *jarīmah* is usually considered similar to the word offence, while crimes of a more serious nature are referred to as *jināyāt* (singular *jināyah*). Petty offences are denoted by the use of the word *ma'siyah*. The emphasis in the words *ḥadd* and *ta'zīr*, on the other hand, is more on the penalty provided rather than on the inherent nature of the act.

We shall deal with these distinctions later in a little more detail. The purpose here was to point the different terms related to the concept of crime. The use of these terms is not uniform in law and even in Islamic law. The position, however, is the same as in the

25. Lewis Mayers, *The American Legal System* (New York, 1964), 11.
26. Ibid.

law with respect to one point: *names alone do not enable us to identify the meaning of an offence,* and we have to examine various attributes of acts designated as crimes and hence offences.

In general discourse it becomes very difficult to maintain a distinction between the terms crime and offence and the words are used as synonyms. This is what the reader will notice in the following pages.

REVIEW QUESTIONS

① What is the difference between the terms "offence" and "crime" in Western law? Does a similar distinction exist in Islamic law as well?

② In order to explain the meaning of crime, what main attributes of a crime can you list? How would you define a crime in the light of these characteristics?

③ Is an offence always a public wrong? What distinctions can you indicate between civil and criminal wrongs?

④ Compare and contrast the positions of Islamic law and Western law when it comes to stating that a crime is always a moral wrong.

⑤ Why are criminal proceedings considered the real test of identifying a crime?

⑥ Should the state try to enforce morality through the criminal law? Compare the position in Western law with that in Islamic law and argue for one of these.

CHAPTER 2

ORIGINS, STRUCTURE AND SOURCES OF THE CRIMINAL LAW

Poverty is the mother of crime.

Marcus Aurelius

2.1 Principles Governing Criminal Law in Pakistan

"The principles of criminal law include many of the ultimate ideas of Western civilization."[27] These principles refined in the last few centuries in the Western world have governed the criminal law of Pakistan since her birth. In the last two decades or so, the criminal law in Pakistan has undergone some change. Major crimes are now governed by the provisions of Islamic law. This means that two sets of principles, one based on divine law and the other on positive law, are operating at the same time in the realm of criminal law. The need to understand the principles of Islamic criminal law in addition to those of Western law is, therefore, immense.

Theoretically, the entire law of crimes stands Islamized in Pakistan. Part of it has been replaced by express provisions of Islamic law. The rest, it is maintained, needs no further amendment, because it is not repugnant to the injunctions of the Qur'ān and the *Sunnah*. If this is correct, the criminal law should now be governed by the general principles of Islamic law rather than those of Western law. Section 338F of the Pakistan Penal Code, inserted with the new law on *qiṣāṣ* and *diyat*, says: "In the interpretation

27. Jerome Hall, *General Principles of Criminal Law* (Indiana: The Bobbs-Merril Company Inc., 1960) vi [herinafter referred to as Jerome Hall, *General Principles*].

and application of the provisions of this Chapter, and in respect of matters ancillary or akin thereto, the court shall be guided by the Injunctions of Islam as laid down in the Holy Qur'ān and Sunnah." This, it is submitted, is a partial application to one chapter alone. If we assert that the entire criminal law has been Islamized, this provision should apply to all the *ta'zīr* offences as well as to each and every provision of the Penal Code. It may be asserted, on the other hand, that there is not much difference between the general principles governing criminal law in the West and those in Islamic law. If it is true, then, this would be all the more reason why the principles of Islamic law should be used.

The assertion that general principles govern the law means that these principles explain the entire law contained in the Penal Code. They elaborate the framework within which each provision of the penal law can be placed and explained. Further, when the judge is not sure about the exact meaning of a particular statute, he has to, or should, fall back on the general principles for an elaboration of the meaning. Today, our judges should rely on the principles and conceptions of Islamic law and not those of Western law—for all provisions of the criminal law. It is only when they do so that the law will be developed and refined in the light of the injunctions of the Qur'ān and the *Sunnah.* Nevertheless, our law colleges and institutions continue to teach the general principles of English law and not to those of Islamic law.

The transition from principles of English law to those of Islamic law may not be very difficult; yet, it requires a thorough analysis and comparison of both sets of principles. A comparative study of the two sets of principles must state clearly how and where the principles are compatible and where they are different. The present study attempts to provide a theoretical, though preliminary, basis for a smooth transition, while meeting fully the needs of the student of criminal law. It is obvious that a fuller treatment is required that runs the whole gamut of the criminal law, including particular crimes.

We begin with an explanation of the structure of the criminal law to show how its propositions, that is, its rules, doctrines and principles operate and interact.

2.2 The Structure of the Criminal Law

Criminal law is constructed around a set of ideas couched in general propositions. Every penal law can be assigned a place within this set and thus explained. Although some of the propositions of criminal law are stated in the Penal Code, in the general part, they cannot be explained in detail there. It is only a study of the general principles of criminal law that makes it possible to distinguish these propositions and to recognize their respective functions as well as their relation to each other.

2.2.1 The propositions of criminal law

The entire penal law can be stated in terms of three types of proposition, each of which serves important distinctive functions.[28]

1. **Principles.** At one extreme, at the apex, are the widest generalizations; namely the "principles" of penal law.
2. **Doctrines.** These are propositions that lack the extensiveness of principles, but are more general than rules. These are stated as general exceptions in the Pakistan Penal Code.
3. **Rules.** These are the narrowest and most numerous of the propositions of criminal law. Rules comprise the specific part of the Penal Code and, in conjunction with the doctrines, they define particular crimes and fix the respective punishments and treatment.

The propositions presently located in the general part of the current code consist of doctrines and principles and other generally applicable "norms," for example those concerning jurisdiction, which while they have general application, are not derived from the rules and doctrines of substantive law.

2.2.2 Functional structure of propositions

More important than the formal structure of the above three types of proposition is their functional difference:

28. Jerome Hall, *General Principles*, 17–18.

1. THE DOCTRINES OF PENAL LAW concern insanity, infancy, intoxication, mistake, coercion, necessity, attempt, conspiracy, abetment by instigation and complicity. The doctrines thus express the common "material" (legally essential) parts of the definitions of specific crimes.
2. As compared to this THE RULES (the special part) state what is distinctive about each crime. But the rules do not exhaust the defintion of these crimes, for example, if the defendant was insane when he caused the injury, no crime was committed by him. Thus, the doctrines are essential in the defintion of the various crimes. The doctrines and the rules combine to give meaning to the definition of a crime or to put it differently, **doctrines must be added to rules to complete the definition of a crime.**

   It is for this reason that §6 of the PPC states:

> Throughout this Code every definition of an offence, every penal provision and every illustration of every such definition or penal provision, shall be understood subject to the exceptions contained in the Chapter entitled "General Exceptions" though those exceptions are not repeated in such definition, penal provision or illustration.
>
> Illustrations
>
> *(a)* The sections of this Code, which contain definitions of offences, do not express that a child under seven years of age cannot commit such offences; but the definitions are to be understood subject to the general exception which provides that nothing shall be an offence which is done by a child under seven years of age.
>
> *(b) A,* a police officer, without warrant, apprehends Z who has committed murder. Here *A* is not guilty of the offence of wrongful confinement; for he was bound by law to apprehend Z, and therefore the case falls within the general exception which provides that "nothing is an offence which is done by a person who is bound by law to do it".

3. *The principles* of criminal law consist of several notions. These are explained in the following section.

2.2.3 The meaning of principles

The principles of criminal law consist of seven ultimate notions expressing (1) *mens rea* (2) act (effort) (3) the "concurrence" (fusion) of *mens rea* and act (4) harm (5) causation (6) punishment and (7) legality. The seven principles can be reduced to three conceptions: law, crime, and punishment. These conceptions are presented by writers in different ways and in different arrangements. This book will deal with them under the following headings:

- The definition of crime.
- The aims of the criminal law—including the justification of punishment and the various theories associated with it.
- The classification of offences.
- The principle of legality—rule of law.
- Criminal liability—*mens rea, actus reus*, and their fusion; and negligence in relation to *mens rea*.
- Crimes of strict liability and vicarious liability.
- Abetment, conspiracy and inchoate crimes.
- General defences—covering most of the doctrines of criminal law.

This arrangement is based upon Western law and not upon Islamic law. It has, however, been selected intentionally, because it will be easier for a reader trained in, or receiving training in, modern law to understand the concepts of Islamic criminal law when these are presented to him within a familiar framework.

2.3 The Sources of Criminal Law in Pakistan

- **The Constitution of Pakistan:** The primary source of the criminal law is the Constititution itself. It lays down that the Qur'ān and the *Sunnah* are the fundamental sources of the law and all laws shall be made in accordance with the injunctions found in them. The Constitution defines the offence of treason and makes provisions for its punishment. In addition to this, a large number of principles governing the laws in general and the criminal law in particular are laid down in the Constitution. For example, Art.9 says: "No person shall be deprived of life or liberty save in accordance with law." Article 10 lays down the following principle:

1. No person who is arrested shall be detained in custody without being informed, as soon as may be of the grounds for such arrest, nor shall he be denied the right to consult and be defended by a legal practitioner of his choice.
2. Every person who is arrested and detained in custody shall be produced before a magistrate within a period of twenty four hours of such arrest,[29] excluding the time necessary for the journey from the place of arrest to the court of the nearest magistrate, and no such person shall be detained in custody beyond the said period without the authority of a magistrate.

There are a number of other principles too, especially those dealing with *ex post facto* laws, and we shall have occasion to refer to such principles during the course of our study.

- **Legislation:** In Pakistan, no crime can be created unless it is legislated and made known to the public. Thus, after the Constitution, legislation is the main source of the criminal law. This includes statutes and even subordinate legislation.
- **General Principles and Doctrines:** These have been incorporated into legislation, but during interpretation of statutes judges are to refer to general principles and doctries, particularly those of the Islamic law. For example, §338-F says: "In the interpretation and application of the provisions of this Chapter, and in respect of matters ancillary or akin thereto, the court shall be guided by the Injunctions of Islam as laid down in the Holy Qur'ān and Sunnah."

29. In many countries this period ranges from 6 to 12 hours. Even the time for Irish terrorists is less than this.

- **Can judges create new crimes?** Judges cannot create new crimes through interpretation of statutes, as these would amount to *ex post facto* laws. In fact, the penal statutes have to be construed strictly. (See section 3.2

2.4 The Pakistan Penal Code: The Nature of Legislation on Criminal Law

One of the major purposes of this book is to compare Western law, or English common law to be more specific, with Islamic law, and the major legislation in the area of crimanal law is the PPC, thus, we need to delve a bit into the background to see what the framers of this important code had to say. We will briefly record two kinds of views from those early times. The first is a quotation from Lord Macauley the official responsible for the drafting of the Pakistan Penal Code (Thomas Babington Macaulay, *Speeches and Poems With the Report and Notes on the Indian Penal Code*, vol. 2 (New York: Hurd & Houghton, 1867)). The other view is about Islamic law given by the Chairman of the East India Company, that is, the top official of the ruling organisation, Archibald Galloway (Archibald Galloway, *Obserations on the Law and Constitution of India: Landed Tenures and Financial Resources*, 2nd ed. (London: Parbury, Allen & Co., 1832)).

2.4.1 Lord McCauley on the Penal Code

Lord Thomas Babington Macaulay was a poet, a great parlimentarian, and the author of the Indian Penal Code (now the Pakistan Penal Code). The following comments are excerpts from the *Introductory Report Upon the Indian Penal Code* to the Right Honourable George Lord Auckland, K. G. C. B., Governor-General of India in Council. The excerpts follow:

"Under the circumstances we have not thought it desirable to take as the groundwork of the code any of the systems of lnw now in force in any part of India. We have, indeed, to the best of our ability, compared the code with all those systems, and we have taken suggestions from all; but we hnve not adopted a single provision merely because it formed a part of any of those systems. We have also compared our work with the most celebrated systems of Western jurisprudence, as far as the very scarity means of information which were accessible to us in this country enabled us to do so. We have derived much valuable assistance from the French code, and from the decisions of the French Courts of Justice on questions touching the construction of that code. We have derived assistance still more valuable from the code of Louisiana, prepared by the late Mr. Livingston. We are the more desirous to acknowledge our obligations to that eminent jurist, because we have found ourselves under the necessity of combatting his opinions on some important questions."[30]

....

"One peculiarity in the manner in which this code is framed will immediately strike your Lordship in Council, we mean the copious use of illustrations. These illustrations will, we trust, greatly facilitate the understanding of the law, and will at the same time often serve as a defence of the law. In our definitions we have repeatedly found ounelves under the necessity of sacrificing neatness and perspicuity to precision, and of using harsh expressions because we could find no other expressions which would convey our whole meaning, and no more than our whole meaning. Such definitions standing by themselves might repel and perplex the reader, and would perhaps be fully comprehended only by a few students after long application. Yet such definitions are found, and must be found, in every system of law which aims at accuracy. A legislator may, if he thinks fit, avoid such definitions, and by avoiding them he will give a smoother and more attractive appearance to his workmanship; but in that case he flinches from a duty which he ought to perform, and which somebody must perform. If this necessary but most disagreeable work be not performed by the lawgiver once for all, it must be constantly performed in a rude and imperfect manner by every judge in the empire, and will probably be performed by no two judges in the same way. We have therefore thought it right not to shrink from the task of framing these unpleasing but indispensable parts of a code. And we hope that when each of these definitions is followed by a collection of cases falling under it, and of cases which, though at first sight they appear to fall under it, do not really fall under it, the definition and the reasons which led to the adoption of it will be readily understood. The illustrations will lead the mind of the student through the same steps by which the minds of those who framed the law proceeded, and may sometimes show him that a phrase which may have struck him as uncouth, or a distinction which he may have thought idle, was deliberately adopted for the purpose of including or excluding a large class of im-

30. Macaulay, *Report on the Indian Penal Code,* vol. 2, 320-21.

portant cases. In the study of geometry it is constantly found that a theorem which, read by itself, connveyed no distinct meaning to the mind, becomes perfectly clear as soon as the reader casts his eye over the statement of the individual case taken for the purpose of demonstration. Our illustrations, we trust, will in a similar manner facilitate the study of the law."

"There are two things which a legislator should always have in view while he is framing laws; the one is, that they should be as far as possible precise: the other, that they should be easily understood. To unite precision and simplicity in definitions intended to indude large classes of things, and to exclude others very similar to many of those which are included, will often be utterly impossible. Under such circumstances it is not easy to say what is the best course. That a law, and especially a penal law, should be drawn in words which convey no meaning to the people who are to obey it is an evil. On the other hand, a loosely-worded law is no law, and to whatever extent a legislature uses vague expressions, to that extent it abdicates its functions, and resigns the power of making law to the Courts of Justice."

"On the whole, we are inclined to think that the best course is that which we have adopted. We have, in framing our definitions, thought principally of making them precise, and have not shrunk from rugged or intricate phraseology when such phraseology appeared to us to be necessary to precision. If it appeared to us that our language was likely to perplex an ordinary reader, we added as many illustrations as we thought necessary for the purpose of explaining it. The definitions and enacting clauses contain the whole law. The illustrations make nothing law which would not be law without them. They only exhibit the law in full action, and show what its effects will be on the events of common life."

"Thus the code will be at once a statute book and a collection of decided cases. The decided cases in the code will differ from the decided cases in the English law books in two most important points. In the first place, our illustrations are never intended to supply any omission in the written law, nor do they ever, in our opinion, put a strain on the written law. They are merely instances of the practical application of the written law to the affairs of mankind. Secondly, they are cases decided not by the judges but by the legislature, by those who make the law, and who must know more certainly than any judge can know what the law is which they mean to make."[31]

31. Ibid., vol. 2, 321-23.

The report by Lord Macauley and the notes to the code are valuable for a deeper study of the code. They should be essential reading for the researcher.

2.4.2 Archibald Galloway on Islamic Law Versus Common Law

Sir Archibald Galloway (1779 1850), was a valiant soldier, later a Major General, a Director of the East India Company, and a writer on military strategy, warfare, and the law in India. In the last year or more of his life, he was chairman of the East India Company; the virtual ruler of India.

And yet, he was an outstanding scholar of Islamic law. He was conversant with Arabic and was at home with the texts of great Ḥanafī jurists like Imam al-Sarakhsī, Qazeekhan and many others. He appears to have mastered the Fatāwā 'Ālamgīrī. The text from which we have excerpted a few paragraphs must be read by all judges, lawyers, police officers, administrators, and revenue officers. It must also be read by the Ulama'. These officials and scholars will find it to be an embarrasing experience: a British ruler of India, who is a master of Islamic law and at home with the classical Arabic manuals on Islamic law. Here he argues for the supremacy of Islamic law and pleads for its application in India in all walks of life.[32] The excerpts follow:

"My opinion of the Moohummudan law may possibly be biased.[33]

32. For a more detailed presentation, see Imran Ahsan Khan Nyazee, *Legal System of Pakistan* (Islamabad: Federal Law House, 2016).
33. Mr. Miller, in his work above-mentioned, has classed me among, if not at the head of, the enthusiastic admirers of the Moohummudan law. It will be nearer the sentiments I entertain on that point to say, that, as a basis of a code for India, I think the Moohummudan law far preferable to any other; and that I admire it as a system of jurisprudence, which admits easily of modification, so as to be more fully applicable to the state of society in India than any other law with which I am acquainted. Moreover, I trust there is some ground for such preference, seeing that the Moohummudan law has actually been the national law of the country for many ages. My knowledge of the Moohummudan law enables me to appreciate its qualities; and

Be that as it may, the rank it holds as the basis of the constitution, as indeed the written law of India, raises the value of that code to an extent that must be fully admitted. An exposition of the Moohummudan law is a desideratum of infinite importance; and I shall be glad to find that any thing I may be able to say here may induce those who have the power, to adopt the measures necessary for cultivating a knowledge of it, so truly indispensable both to those who legislate for, and those who administer the laws to, the people of India. Were it, indeed, of no other use but as an exercise for the intellect, the study of the Moohummudan law would be intrinsically valuable. I will venture to say, that no one can study with attention a good treatise on the Moohummudan law, without having his reasoning faculties improved."

"With respect to the English law, and its fitness to be either made a part of or to supersede entirely the ancient law of India, it is necessary for me to say something. In Mr. Mill's estimation, the law of England has very much suffered in comparison with the Moohummudan code. But Mr. Mill is not the first that has expressed an unfavourable opinion of the English law. It has often been censured by Englishmen of the greatest wisdom and experience. What encouragement, then, have we to transplant it into India? The English have, in fact, no regular code of law. A multiplicity of statutes they have, indeed; but they are unintelligible to many, most of them altered or partially revoked, many altogether rescinded, so that an English gentleman knows not where to look for law.[34] He is, therefore, compelled on every occasion to refer to a practitioner; and this practitioner refers not to any standard authorized by the constitutional legislature of England, but to a body of decisions on particular cases, which have been passed from time to time in the courts, by men, some of whom were wise, and some perhaps not so 'full of wisdom,' but whose said decisions have, in fact, now become the law of England."

"Such law being founded upon no general principles, but piled up, as it were, upon particular cases as they arose, must ever be uncertain, because there can be no two cases, occurring at different periods, precisely similar in every point of view: and, at best, it is but a crude mode of lawmaking. It is a kind of *ex post facto* manufacture, which must ever have been influenced, in some degree, by the peculiar circumstances of

---

to see that it is free from many imperfections usually ascribed to it.

34. Let those who advocate the introduction of English law into India, look at the demolition it is undergoing at home. Are we to take for India what the people of England are so eagerly rejecting? At all events, let us see what is suffered to remain of English law, in England, before we import it into India.

the parties to the case on which the decision was passed, as well as by the sentiments and feelings of the times."

"This mode of legislation is completely reversing the order of things. The duty of a judge is to explain and to administer, not to make laws."

"The English criminal law is by a Moohummudan lawyer esteemed barbarous in the extreme. It certainly has ever been found inadequate to the purpose for which it was designed. It has failed to check crime; and only by the permission of Providence has it succeeded in peopling the wilds of America and New Holland. Its severity has become latterly the means of rendering it in many cases a dead letter. The feelings of the people are inimical to it; and the officers of the Crown have often failed, notwithstanding the clearest evidence, to get the constitutional tribunals to convict under it."[35]

"A Moohummudan lawyer would naturally ask, upon what principle is it that the life of a human being should be taken away for stealing the value of a few pieces of silver, when the most notorious adulterer and seducer, the destroyer, perhaps, not of the life, but certainly of the honour, peace, and happiness, not only of the individual more immediately injured, but of whole families, is suffered to pass unpunished by the law, nay, to live openly in the sin of adultery, in the face of all mankind?"

"He would also ask, on what principle is the severity of the law of forgery founded? Why is a man to suffer death for making an imitation of one thing which has no real value (a scrawl or engraving upon a bit of worthless paper), when he may imitate every thing else of value which the same person possesses? He may imitate even his best invention, and utter it with the intention of defrauding the inventor. If the inventor has obtained a protection for his invention, the imitator is at most liable only to a fine. If no protection has been obtained, the imitator has acted legally, though he has defrauded the other perhaps of thousands: but if he thus imitate and sell, that is, issue his note for twenty shillings, he is hanged. This is, probably, the mode of reasoning which a man, ignorant of the feelings prevalent in our commercial country, would advance."

"The Moohummudan lawyer will think farther. He will refer to his own law, and there he will find that it is the duty of every owner of property to adopt proper and effectual means of a physical nature, sufficient (generally speaking) to secure his property. If he have not done this, its abstraction from him, though a misdemeanor, is not theft, under the statute. Analogy would therefore immediately suggest to a Moslem, that

35. It will be recollected, that since the first edition of this work was published, many important alterations have been introduced into the law of England.

if an individual, or body of individuals, shall choose to create a property on a bit of worthless paper, and that that property shall be found from experience not to be under that degree of protection which is required by law over all other property, but to be constantly exposed as the easiest prey, as notes are, by being so easily forged, he would immediately conclude that such property is not sufficiently guarded by its owner, and consequently is without the protection of the law."

....

"A Moohummudan lawyer, were he to sit down and compare his own law with ours, would no doubt pay us home, by developing all our legal deformities, as we have with very great pains done the foibles of his law. Nor would he estimate, perhaps, so highly as we do its excellencies. Even its two great and pre-eminent towers, the habeas corpus and the trial by jury, might not extract any uncommon eulogium. He would approve of the former, because, by his own law, every judge is not only empowered to inquire into the state of prisons, and into the case of all prisoners, but he is strictly enjoined, above all things, to visit the jails, and to enquire personally of every individual the grounds of his confinement and nature of his case, and to give him relief according to law. A most merciful law it is too, compared with the English. I say he would approve of the Habeas Corpus; but he would tell us that but for this statute, of which we boast so much, we should be no better than slaves, who might, at the nod of our master, be imprisoned, to remain during his pleasure; and that, after all, it was no great matter to boast of, that we were not slaves."

....

"Upon the whole, the learned Moslem would add, permit me to say, that although our law, having been framed for a state of society now no more, is doubtless defective, it is nevertheless not inferior to yours; and farther (which is of greater importance), it contains principles which will admit of its improvement and extension, so as to become applicable to the change of the times; and which principles, if judiciously applied, might, without destroying or even injuring its original fabric, be made the basis of a code that should hold a high place even in your own estimation: a far more perfect code than those who know it not can believe. If you desire to legislate for this empire, forget not this! Do not despise the wisdom of our God and yours; of our prophet, of our holy men, of our forefathers, which has been the guide of our actions here, and is the source of our hopes hereafter, the standard by which our ideas, our morals, and those of our fellow-subjects (though religious foes) have for ages of ages been formed, the very bond which unites society. If you take away this, we shall no longer know in what relation we stand to one another. A father will not know the propinquity of his child, nor the child that of his father; a husband that of his wife, a wife that of her husband: a law which age has rendered venerable, both to the believer and the unbeliever. As you are humane, you will preserve and reverence it, for its own sake and ours; as you are wise, you will preserve and improve it for your own. You cannot change the law of any country for that of any other, even for a better, without offering great violence to the people: to the people of India above all others."[36]

Review Questions

① What is the meaning of "principles" in the context of criminal law?

② Distinguish between "principles," "doctrines," and "rules" of criminal law.

③ What do we mean when we say that the doctrines have to be added to the meaning of rules to arrive at the definition of a crime?

④ Identify the seven main notions of the criminal law and discuss why they are considered important.

⑤ Has the entire criminal law been Islamized? If it has, should we refer only to the principles of Islamic criminal law?

⑥ What in your view are the implications of §338F that requires interpretation of certain provisions in the light of the injunctions of the Qur'ān and the *Sunnah*.

⑦ What are the sources of criminal law in Pakistan?

36. Nyazee, *Legal System of Pakistan*, 297–304.

CHAPTER 3

CRIMINAL LAW AND THE CONSTITUTION

A criminal is a person with predatory instincts who has not sufficient capital to form a corporation.

Howard Scott

The power to enact criminal laws was on the concurrent list shared by the federation and the provinces. The concurrent list was abolished by the 18th amendment to the Constitution, however, the same amendment inserted Article 142 (b), which states the following: "Majlis-e-Shoora (Parliament) and a Provincial Assembly shall have power to make laws with respect to criminal law, criminal procedure and evidence."[37] The PPC, the CrPC and the Evidence Act are, therefore, still under concurrent power.

In democratic countries, legislative bodies are, theoretically, supreme in enacting statutes defining crimes and providing penalties. The only superior or overarching authority is the will of the people manifested through the ballot box.[38] The Constitution limits the power of the legislatures. To remove these restrictions, the Constitution needs to be amended. The Constitution places restrictions from the perspective of Islam and Islamic law as well. The Islamic provisions of the Constitution may, therefore, be considered as restrictions on the enactment of criminal law and the law of evidence as well. These restrictions are implemented through the power of judicial review that the superior courts possess; they will strike down laws that defy these restrictions. [39]

37. Pakistan Constitution, art. 142 (b).
38. Scheb and II, *Criminal Law and Procedure,* 51.
39. "In addressing constitutional assaults on criminal statutes, courts are sometimes asked to declare that a statute is unconstitutional under any circumstances, whereas in other instances a court might simply

The Constitution is not only a source of restrictions, but also a source of the criminal law. We may, therefore, list some of the articles that are concerned directly or indirectly with the criminal law. After that we will look at the principle of legality that is linked to the rule of law.

3.1 Significant Articles of the Constitution

3.1.1 Article on Rule of Law

Articles 4 and 5 deal with the rule of law. They deal with rights and duties that are viewed outside the context of fundamental rights; they have an independent existence. Article 4 emphasises that all persons—rich or poor, strong or weak, male or female—must be treated equally by the law, and must receive equal protection. Further, no one is to be taken to task for something that is not prohibited by law. Article 5 talks about the duties owed by the citizen to the state in terms of obedience to the law.

Art. 4. Right of individuals to be dealt with in accordance with law, etc.—(1) To enjoy the protection of law and to be treated in accordance with law is the inalienable right of every citizen, wherever he may be, and of every other person for the time being within Pakistan.

(2) In particular—

(a) no action detrimental to the life, liberty, body, reputation or property of any person shall be taken except in accordance with law;

---

be asked to rule that the statute cannot constitutionally apply to certain conduct. A statute may be declared unconstitutional *per se* in that it inherently trenches on some constitutionally protected liberty or exceeds the constitutional powers of government. For example, a law that would restrict citizens' freedom to profess their religious beliefs would be inherently unconstitutional. Alternatively, a law that is facially valid, such as an ordinance prohibiting disorderly conduct, may be declared unconstitutional as applied if it is enforced in a way that impermissibly restricts or punishes the exercise of constitutional rights." Scheb and II, *Criminal Law and Procedure,* 52.

(b) no person shall be prevented from or be hindered in doing that which is not prohibited by law; and

(c) no person shall be compelled to do that which the law does not required him to do.

Art. 5. Loyalty to State and obedience to Constitution and law.—(1) Loyalty to the State is the basic duty of every citizen.

(2) Obedience to the Constitution and law is the inviolable obligation of every citizen wherever he may be and of every other person for the time being within Pakistan.

3.1.2 High Treason

This is the highest form of crime insofar as it attempts to demolish the whole system.

Art. 6. High treason.—(1) Any person who abrogates or subverts or suspends or holds in abeyance, or attempts or conspires to abrogate or subvert or suspend or hold in abeyance, the Constitution by use of force or show of force or by any other unconstitutional means shall be guilty of high treason.

(2) Any person aiding or abetting or collaborating the acts mentioned in clause (1) shall likewise be guilty of high treason. (2A) An act of high treason mentioned in clause (1) or clause (2) shall not be validated by any court including the Supreme Court and a High Court.

(3) Majlis-e-Shoora (Parliament) shall by law provide for the punishment of persons found guilty of high treason.

3.1.3 Laws Against Fundamental Rights Void

As far as the criminal law is concerned, the article implies that no act is to be declared a crime, if it is against the fundamental rights granted by the Constitution. It appears that in case of a clash of this article with Article 2A, the Islamic provision will prevail, but the Courts have not spelled out this rule clearly.

Art. 8. Laws inconsistent with or in derogation of Fundamental Rights to be void.—(1) Any law, or any custom or usage having the force of law, in so far as it is inconsistent with the rights conferred by this Chapter, shall, to the extent of such inconsistency, be void.

(2) The State shall not make any law which takes away or abridges the rights so conferred and any law made in contravention of this clause shall, to the extent of such contravention, be void.

(3) The provisions of this Article shall not apply to—

(a) any law relating to members of the Armed Forces, or of the police or of such other forces as are charged with the maintenance of public order, for the purpose of ensuring the proper discharge of their duties or the maintenance of discipline among them; or

(b) any of the—

(i) laws specified in the First Schedule as in force immediately before the commencing day or as amended by any of the laws specified in that Schedule;

(ii) other laws specified in Part I of the First Schedule;

and no such law nor any provision thereof shall be void on the ground that such law or provision is inconsistent with, or repugnant to, any provision of this Chapter.

(4) Notwithstanding anything contained in paragraph (b) of clause (3), within a period of two years from the commencing day, the appropriate Legislature shall bring the laws specified in Part II of the First Schedule into conformity with the rights conferred by this Chapter:

Provided that the appropriate Legislature may by resolution extend the said period of two years by a period not exceeding six months.

Explanation.—If in respect of any law Majlis-e-Shoora (Parliament) is the appropriate Legislature, such resolution shall be a resolution of the National Assembly.

(5) The rights conferred by this Chapter shall not be suspended except as expressly provided by the Constitution.

3.1.4 Security of Life and Liberty

Justifiable homicide, for example, pertains to this Article.

Art. 9. Security of person.—No person shall be deprived of life or liberty save in accordance with law.

3.1.5 Safeguards as to Arrest and Detention

Art. 10. Safeguards as to arrest and detention.—(1) No person who is arrested shall be detained in custody without being informed, as soon as may be, of the grounds for such arrest, nor shall he be denied the right to consult and be defended by a legal practitioner of his choice.

(2) Every person who is arrested and detained in custody shall be produced before a magistrate within a period of twenty-four hours of such arrest, excluding the time necessary for the journey from the place of arrest to the court of the nearest magistrate, and no such person shall be detained in custody beyond the said period without the authority of a magistrate.

(3) Nothing in clauses (1) and (2) shall apply to any person who is arrested or detained under any law providing for preventive detention.

(4) No law providing for preventive detention shall be made except to deal with persons acting in a manner prejudicial to the integrity, security or defence of Pakistan or any part thereof, or external affairs of Pakistan, or public order, or the maintenance of supplies or services, and no such law shall authorise the detention of a person for a period exceeding three months unless the appropriate Review Board has, after affording him an opportunity of being heard in person, reviewed his case and reported, before the expiration of the said period, that there is, in its opinion, sufficient cause for such detention, and, if the detention is continued after the said period of 1three months, unless the appropriate Review Board has reviewed his case and reported, before the expiration of each perio

There are other clauses for this article that have not been reproduced.

3.1.6 Right to Fair Trial and Due Process

The jurisprudence of due process is yet to be developed fully by the Courts. Some guidance may be sought from the U.S. rules about substantive and procedural due process.

Art. 10A. Right to fair trial.—For the determination of his civil rights and obligations or in any criminal charge against him a person shall be entitled to a fair trial and due process.

3.1.7 No Retrospective Punishment

This is one reason why judges cannot make criminal laws through their judgements, as in that case they would be deciding retrospectively.

Art. 12. Protection against retrospective punishment.—(1) No law shall authorize the punishment of a person—

(a) for an act or omission that was not punishable by law at the time of the act or omission; or

(b) for an offence by a penalty greater than, or of a kind different from, the penalty prescribed by law for that offence at the time the offence was committed.

(2) Nothing in clause (1) or in Article 270 shall apply to any law making acts of abrogation or subversion of a Constitution in force in Pakistan at any time since the twenty-third day of March, one thousand nine hundred and fifty-six, an offence.

3.1.8 Double Jeopardy and Self-Incrimination

Art. 13. Protection against double punishment and self-incrimination.—No person—

(a) shall be prosecuted or punished for the same offence more than once; or

(b) shall, when accused of an offence, be compelled to be a witness against himself.

Accordingly, section 403 of the Criminal Procedure Code, begins as follows:

403. Person once convicted or acquitted not to be tried for same offence.—(1) A person who has once been tried by a Court of competent jurisdiction for an offence and convicted or acquitted of such offence shall, while such conviction or acquittal remains in force, not be liable to be tried again for the same offence, nor on the same facts for any other offence for which a different charge from the one made against him might have been made under section 236, or for which he might have been convicted under section 237.

3.2 Legality: *Nulla Poena Sine Lege*

The principle of legality—the rule of law—is designed to protect individual interests guaranteed by a society by bringing into effect limitations on the power of the state.[40] The principle requires three things:

- A body of governing legal precepts.
- Institutions vested with appropriate legal power to apply these rules.
- Determined legal procedures by which the precepts may be applied by the institutions.

While discussing the principle, many writers on the subject stress the procedural connotations of the principle, especially the fairness of the trial and the independence of the judiciary.[41] What is seldom emphasized is the historic meaning of the principle of legality as a definite limitation on the power of the state.[42] Limitation on the power of the state is the central meaning of the principle in penal law.

The primary and formal function of the principle of legality **is to provide a distinction between penal laws and all other positive laws.** This distinction is reflected in the general meaning of the principle and its two corollaries as follows.

1. When we focus on punsihment, that is, **poena,** the principle requires that *no person may be punished except in pursuance of a statute that prescribes a penalty*. This is stated in Latin as *nulla poena sine lege*.

40. Jerome Hall, *General Principles of Criminal Law,* 27.
41. Ibid.
42. Ibid.

2. When we focus on the act that is declared as an offence, the principle requires that *no conduct may be held as criminal unless it is precisely described in a penal law.* This is the meaning of the principle *nullum crimen sine lege.*
3. To sharpen our understanding of the meanings at (1) and (2), the following corollaries are also stated:

   a) Penal statutes must be strictly construed.
   b) Penal statutes must not be given retroactive effect.

All these meanings work against the wide powers that a state may wish to enjoy by insisting that the purpose of the criminal law is "to punish socially dangerous conduct by any sanction which the judge deems proper." Thus, the principle requires that: rules declaring conduct to be criminal must be stated specifically; the rules must be construed strictly; and the rules must be applied to acts committed after the declaration of acts as criminal.

Before we discuss some of the details of these meanings it would suit our purposes to briefly trace the history of the principle in the West.

3.2.1 Brief history of the principle

The principle of legality has a chequered history. Some writers maintain that even though the principle is stated in Latin, it is really a product of eighteenth century liberalism. Traces of the principle, however, can be found in Roman law, especially in the laws applied by Sulla[43] and Augustus.[44]

In the Middle Ages, the principle was almost non-existent. There are writers who try to read the meaning of the principle into the Magna Carta, but others deny this. In England, the principle became prominent in the Charter of Henry the First (ruled 1100–1135 A.D.). After this the principle is visible in the writings of Bracton and it played a major role in the rise of the Parliament.[45]

43. Lucius Cornellius Sulla 138–78 B.C. He was a Roman general and dictator.
44. 63 B.C–14 A.D. He was the first Roman Emperor.
45. Jerome Hall, *General Principles of Criminal Law,* 31–32.

In the rest of Europe, the principle was not accepted till the early part of the 18th century. Thus, the Prussian Code of 1721, the Bavarian Code of 1751 and the Austrian Code of 1769 had provisions that went against the principle of legality. Its first clear expression is found in the Code of Joseph II (1787), the Austrian monarch. Two years later, the principle was stated in the Virginia declaration of 1789 (eighth article) in America. The principle was stated in the French constitution of 1791 and in the Penal Code of 1810. This Code became the model for the rest of Europe and the principle was accepted generally in the 19th century.[46]

The famous German philosopher Ludwig Andreas von Feuerbach (1804–72) is credited with the statement of the principle as we find it today in Western legal systems. It was he who used the phrases: *nulla poena sine lege, nulla poena sine crimine,* and *nullum crimen sine poena lagali.* He advocated strict adherence to statute and rejected analogy.

3.2.2 Origins of the principle in Islam

In Islamic law the meaning of the principle was stated clearly in the Qur'ān. The following verses higlight this meaning:

1. وما كنّا معذّبين حتّي نبعث رسولا

   "Nor would We visit with our wrath until we had sent a messenger (to give warning)."[47] This verse emphasizes the element of punishment, the poena.

2. وما كان ربّك مهلك القري حتّي يبعث في أمّها رسولا يتلوا عليهم آياتنا

   "Nor was thy Lord the one to destroy a population until He had sent to its centre a messenger, rehearsing to them Our signs."[48] The implication

46. Ibid. 32–34.
47. Qur'ān 17 : 15
48. Qur'ān 28 : 59

of this verse is more or less the same as the first verse.

3. قُل لِّلَّذِينَ كَفَرُوا إِن يَنتَهُوا يُغْفَرْ لَهُم مَّا قَدْ سَلَفَ

"Say to the unbelievers, if (now) they desist, their past would be forgiven them."[49] This verse implies that retroactive punishment will not be awarded.

On the basis of these verses, modern Arab writers state the principle in Arabic as

لا جريمة ولا عقوبة بلا نص

There can be no crime and no punishment without a text (statute)

This, however, appears to be a literal translation of

Nullum crimen nulla poena sine lege

Nevertheless, we can see that the basis for the principle is laid down in the Qur'ān.

The principle has been followed strictly in the case of *ḥudūd* penalties and for *qiṣāṣ*. For these crimes, the Qur'ān itself has prescribed penalties, except in the case of drinking *khamr* (wine) for which the penalty is provided in the *Sunnah*. For *ta'zīr* offences, on the other hand, the record is not very commendable in the light of this principle, and the writings of some jurists suggest that *ta'zīr* crimes as well as suitable punishments could be created at the discretion of the *qāḍī* himself. This, however, appears to be the interpretation of that age. In the light of the principles set out in the Qur'ān, all offences and sentences must be given a statutory form before they are applied.

3.2.3 Main Implications of the Principle

The main requirements of the principle, as practiced in various legal systems, are briefly reproduced below:

49. Qur'ān 8 : 38

3.2.3.1 The void-for-vagueness rule

In the United States the "due process clause" has been interpreted by the Supreme Court to require that no criminal penalty be imposed without fair notice that the conduct is forbidden. Called the "void-for-vagueness" rule, it implies two things:

1. **Fair Warning:** A criminal statute must give a person of ordinary intelligence fair notice that his contemplated conduct is forbidden by the statute.

2. **Arbitrary and Discriminatory Enforcement Must Be Avoided:** A statute must not encourage arbitrary and erratic arrests and convictions.

In Pakistan today, it is necessary to focus on the element of "fair warning." The fair warning element implies that criminal laws should be clearly understood by the people or ordinary intelligence. Unfortunately, many of the laws contained in the Penal Code as well as those scattered over other statutes are not understood by the masses. Some, in fact, are of a highly technical nature. (See, eg, the discussion under abetment on pages 148 and 158). These offences are based on the British laws, which have grown out of British culture and are stated in terminology with which the British people are familiar. For the people in Pakistan, these are alien laws and alien concepts. It is suggested that the criminal law should be simplified and stated in language that has some meaning for the masses. This applies to the substantive law as well as the procedural law. Further, it is the task of the television services in Pakistan to promote an understanding of the criminal law.

3.2.3.2 Constitutional limitations on crime creation

In general the constitutions of different countires place two substantive limitations on legislatures.

1. **No Ex Post Facto Laws:** The Constitution of Pakistan provides in article 12 that no *ex post facto* laws laws shall be

made.[50] An *ex post facto* law is one that operates retroactively to:

a) Make criminal an act that when done was not criminal;

b) Aggravate a crime or increase the punishment therefor;

c) Change the rules of evidence to the detriment of criminal defendants as a class; or

d) Alter the law of criminal procedure to deprive criminal defendants of a substantive right.

2. **No infliction of punishment or denial of privilege without trial:** These are generally referred to as bills of attainder in the U.S. A bill of attainder is a legislative act that inflicts punishment or denies a privilege without a judicial trial. Although a bill of attainder may also be an *ex post facto* law, a distinction can be drawn in that an *ex post facto* law does not deprive the offender of a judicial trial.

3.2.3.3 The criminal statutes are to be construed strictly

1. **The Plain Meaning Rule is to be Followed:** When the statutory language is plain and its meaning clear, the court must give effect to it even if the court feels that the law is unwise or undesirable. An exception to this rule exists if the court believes that to apply the plain meaning of a statute will lead to injustice, oppression, or an absurd consequence. In Islamic law, the Ḥanafīs do not permit the extension of the meaning of *khamr* to other "intoxicants" through a liberal interpretation. The offence for using intoxicants is proved through other texts that mention intoxicants expressly. Thus, they

50. Article 12(1) says:

No law shall authorize the punishment of a person-

(a) for an act or omission that was not punishable by law at the time of the act or omission; or

(b) for an offence by a penalty greater than, or of a kind different from, the penalty prescribed by law for that offence at the time the offence was committed.

have derived two offences from such an act. The Prohibition Order in Pakistan has, however, followed the majority opinion contrary to the plain meaning rule.

2. **Analogy Cannot be Used to Extend Crimes:** This rule is upheld in the law as well as in Islamic law. The Ḥanafī jurists insist that *qiyās* cannot be used to extend the scope of crimes. For example, the offence of drinking *khamr* cannot be extended through analogy.

3. **Ambiguous Statutes Strictly Construed in Favour of Defendant:** This rule requires that an ambiguous criminal statute must be strictly construed in favour of the defendant. Ambiguity should be distinguished from vagueness mentioned above. An ambiguous statute is one susceptible to two or more equally reasonable interpretations. A vague statute is one that is so unclear as to be susceptible to no reasonable interpretation.

4. **Expressio Unius, Exclusio Alterius:** According to this maxim, the expression of one thing impliedly indicates an intention to exclude another.

   §494 PPC prohibits remarriage by one who has a living spouse when such marriage is void during the lifetime of the existing spouse. The statute expressly provides an exception for one whose spouse disappeared more than seven years before. Can a person remarry if the spouse has been gone for less than seven years provided he or she believes in good faith that the spouse is dead? The answer is no. The fact that the statute provides one exception impliedly excludes all others.

5. **The Specific Controls the General, the More Recent Controls the Earlier:** If two statutes address the same subject matter but dictate different conclusions, the more specific statute will be applied rather than the more general. The more recently enacted statute will control an older statute.

> If one statute prohibits all forms of gambling and another permits charity-sponsored raffles, the later will control a church raffle.
>
> A 1980 statute banning advertising of cigarettes will govern a 1975 statute providing a limit on advertising expenditure by cigarette manufacturers.

3.2.3.4 Effect of repeal

At common law, in the absence of a saving provision, the repeal or invalidation of a statute operates to bar prosecutions for earlier violations, provided the prosecution is pending or not yet under way at the time of the repeal. However, a repeal will not operate to set free a person who has been prosecuted and convicted and as to whom the judgment has become final. Codes usually include a provision to the effect that crimes committed prior to the effective date of the new code are subject to prosecution and punishment under the law as it existed at the time the offence was committed (see 338-H in the PPC).

REVIEW QUESTIONS

① Elaborate the meaning of the principle *nullum crimen nulla poena sine lege* and discuss its implication.

② Does the principle of legality as applied to criminal law exist in Islam? Highlight its sources and explain their implications.

③ How does the Constitution of Pakistan give expression to the principle of legality?

④ What is the relationship between the principle of legality and analogy? Discuss from the perspective of Western law as well as Islamic law?

⑤ What effect does the principle of legality have on the interpretation of statutes? Provide details from Western law and Islamic law.

⑥ What effect does the principle of legality have on the interpretation of statutes.

CHAPTER 4

CLASSIFICATION OF OFFENCES

The greater the number of laws and enactments, the more thieves and robbers there will be.

Lao-tzu

The classification of crimes is not a very important topic within the context of general principles of criminal law, but for Islamic law it may be of crucial significance. The classification of crimes in Islamic law helps us understand the structure of the Islamic criminal law and to appreciate the underlying reasoning adopted by the *fuqahā'*. We shall briefly trace the growth of Anglo-American literature[51] on the criminal law to see how crimes were classified, and then take up in some detail the classification of crimes in Islamic law alongwith the ensuing problems in modern times.

4.1 Classification of Crimes in Western Law

We shall first look at the earlier classifications of crimes in Western law and then examine a modern classification that is generally accepted. The earlier classifications will help us compare them with classifications in Islamic law.

4.1.1 Earlier classifications

4.1.1.1 Bracton

In England the first writer on criminal law is considered to be Bracton. He was called "the crown and flower of English medieval ju-

51. We will be relying mostly on the work of Jerome Hall for this purpose.

risprudence." A large number of terms that are used in the criminal law were first employed by him: robbers, burglars, thieves, forgers, treason, conspirators, sedition, homicide, breaking the peace, mayhem, assault, abortion, false-imprisonment. There was no classification of crimes in his writings and the lines of analysis were procedural.

4.1.1.2 Hale

The next great work was by Hale (*Hale's Pleas of the Crown*) towards the end of the seventeenth century (published posthumously around 1736). Hale classified crimes as follows:

1. Crimes against God
2. Crimes against man
    a) Capital offences: treason; offences against life of man; larceny; robbery; and piracy.
    b) Non-capital offences

Exactly the same classification was adopted by Hawkins in 1716 (*Pleas of the Crown, 1716*), but his work published before Hale's book is considered by some as plagiarism, because it is very closely modelled after Hale's work. It is Hale's work that is considered the greatest accomplishment of any single scholar in the field.

We may point out here that the classification adopted by Hale has striking similarities with the classification adopted by Muslim jurists centuries earlier. Hale also discussed in the general part matters like punishments, incapacities (infancy, idiocy, insanity), accident, ignorance of law and of fact, compulsion and necessity. All these matters were discussed in detail by Muslim jurists not only under the criminal law, but also under the general theory of liability in *uṣūl al-fiqh*. It has also been suggested that the doctrine of assizes in nothing but the doctrine of *siyāsah*.[52] It is possible

52. This has been suggested by John Maqdisi in an article published around 1990. Unfortunately, I do not have the title of the article with

that all these ideas went to England from Ottoman Turkey. The idea here is not to claim some kind of superiority for Islamic criminal law, but show that the Muslim jurists had done their part in the development of the law. Those who accuse the early jurists of falling prey to *taqlīd* are the ones who are guilty of not developing the law further and of falling prey to the forces of colonization.

Hale is accused of concentrating more on particular statutes, specific cases and procedural questions as compared to the time devoted to the general part. A similar allegation is levelled against Muslim jurists not only for the criminal law, but also for the law of contracts and the law of torts. These allegations can only be levelled from our present vantage point, but in those days both were considered workable systems of law. Further, the Muslim jurists elaborated the theoretical structure within *uṣūl al-fiqh* rather than in individual branches.

4.1.1.3 Blackstone

Hales' work was followed by Blackstone's *Commentaries*. Blackstone borrowed from the works of European writers like Grotius, Pufendorf, Domat, Beccaria and Montesquieu, and he is not considered an original writer. His work, however, left the criminal law of England not only better organized than he found it but also in a state, which for the most part, is even now generally accepted.

me at present. In any case, those who understand the doctrine of *siyāsah* need only look at the dictionary meaning of the word assize to notice the similarities. The dictionary definition is: *to sit beside, assist in the office of the qāḍī; an enactment made by the legislative assembly: ordinance; a statute regulating weights and measures of articles sold in the market; the regulation of the price of bread or ale by the price of grain; a judicial inquest; the former periodical sessions of the superior courts in English counties for trial of civil and criminal cases....* It can easily be noticed that all these functions are included in the *siyāsah* jurisdiction of the state or *imām*.

4.1.1.4 East, Russel, and Gabbet

The next writer was East (1863), who focused mostly on specific offences. Russel (1819) followed Blackstone as regards general concepts, but he relegated crimes against religion or against God to merely three pages. Gabbet (1835) also followed Blackstone's arrangement. This stage may be taken to be the turning point as classifications on the basis of the right of God were given less importance.

4.1.1.5 Bentham, Austin, Stephen and Kenny

Most of the principal concepts of current criminal law, however, were analyzed in the writings of Bentham, Austin, Stephen and Kenny. Stephen said:

> [S]ince the publication of Blackstone's *Commentaries* hardly any work has been published in England upon the Criminal law which aims at being more than a book of practice, and books of practice on Criminal Law are simply compilations of extracts from text-writers, and reports arranged with greater or less skill—usually with almost none...."[53]

These words can be applied to the state of criminal law in Pakistan today, with the difference that there are absolutely no text-writers on the subject. The result is that we do not know how far the law in this country lags behind that in other common-law countries or how it has deviated from current criminal law in England. The Law Commission does publish its reports, and no independent analysis has ever been published in the form of an authoritative text.

53. Stephen, H. Cr. L. 218–19 (1883) as quoted in Jerome Hall, *Criminal Law*, 10 n. 22.

4.1.1.6 American writers

Among the American writers, the well known are Wharton (1816), Bishop (1856) and Oliver Wendell Holmes. *The Common Law* by Holmes presents an excellent analysis of certain basic issues.

The result of the description provided is that for two centuries crimes were classified into those against God or religion and those against man. It is only in current times that the emphasis may have shifted. We find that this classification undertaken in the last few centuries is no different, in its broad features, from the classification adopted by Muslim *fuqhā'*.

4.2 Classification of Crimes in Islamic Law

Muslim jurists classified crimes on basis of the right violated. These, as stated earlier, were the rights of Allah, the rights of the individual, the rights of Allah mixed with the rights of the individual. The last category was divided into two types depending on whether it was the right of Allah that was predominant or the right of the individual. In fact, Muslim jurists classified all laws on this pattern. The classification on the basis of rights is linked directly with procedure. The kind of right violated determines the procedure to be followed in courts. If the right of Allah is violated, the procedure followed is that for *ḥudūd* and *qiṣāṣ*. When the right of the individual is violated, the procedure followed is that prescribed for *ta'zīr,* which maintains the *nisāb* in evidence of two females for one male. When the right of the state is violated, the procedure followed is that of *siyāsah.*

4.2.1 Classification on the basis of the right affected: *ḥadd, ta'zīr* and *siyāsah*

Jurists like al-Sarakhsī placed *ḥudūd* penalties, excluding the *ḥadd* of *qadhf* in the category of the pure right of Allah. The *ḥadd* of *qadhf* is classified as a mixture of the right of Allah and the right of the individual, in which the right of Allah is predominant. The offence of murder liable to *qiṣāṣ* is classified as a mixture of the right of Allah and the right of the individual, but here it is the right of the indiviudal that is predominant. *Ta'zīr* and *diyah* are classified by most Ḥanafī jurists as belonging to the area of the right of the individual. The *fuqahā'* do not mention the *siyāsah* penalties, yet we know that the ruler exercised this jurisdiction right from the first century of the Hijrah onwards. The *maẓālim* courts, the institution of the *'āmil al-sūq*, and the institution of the *muḥtasib* belong to this jurisdiction. This was the are of the right of the state. Let us list these areas before proceeding further:

1. **The right of Allah**: The *Ḥudūd* offences excluding the *ḥadd* of *qadhf*.
2. **Mixed right—right of Allah predominant:** The *ḥadd* of *qadhf*. According to the Shāfi'īs, *qadhf* is a pure right of the individual.
3. **Mixed right—right of the individual predominant:** The offence of murder punishable with *qiṣāṣ*.
4. **Right of the indiviudal:** *Diyāt* and *ta'zīr*. It is to be noted that offences under *ta'zīr* have a very limited scope in the system devised by the jurists.
5. **Right of the state:** All the offences determined and defined through the *ijtihād* of the ruler, according to a defined methodology, adjudicated through a procedure determined by the state.

The classification of laws into those invoking the right of Allah and those related to the right of the individual is not an idle classification. The Muslim jurists were not fond of classification for the sake of classification, as some critics assume. This classification makes a great difference in practice. Indeed, it is the most important classification in the Islamic legal system. It has tremendous explanatory power as far as the structure of the legal system is concerned. Many important consequences flow from it. We shall only mention a few of these with reference to the Islamic law of crimes. This classification may also be used to point out the distinction between *ḥadd* and *ta'zīr*, although the jurists have pointed out a number of other distinctions too. The consequences of this classification for Islamic Criminal Law are the following:

1. **Commuting the sentence and pardon:** The penalty for an offence against the right of Allah cannot be waived or commuted after apprehension and conviction. However, the penalty for an offence against the right of an individual alone or against the rights of individuals, that is, the right of the state, can be commuted. The important point to be made here is that if the right of Allah and the right of the state (or the right of the community as a whole) were the same thing, the state would not be able to commute any sentence according to the system developed by the jurists, whether awarded as *ḥadd, ta'zīr*, or as *siyāsah*. We know very well that the state can pardon any sentence that is not a *ḥadd*. The reason is that sentences other than *ḥadd* are not awarded and applied as a right of Allah.

2. **The operation of *shubhāt* (mistakes) in *ḥudūd*:** *Shubhah* (lit. doubt) in the right of Allah has the effect of waiving the penalty of *ḥadd*, while it does not have the same effect in *ta'zīr*. *Qiṣāṣ* (retaliation) has been assigned an element of the right of Allah as it is waived due to *shubhah*. This kind of doubt is not to be confused with the benefit of a doubt that goes to the accused in positive law, which is a doubt in the mind of the judge as to whether the crime has been proved beyond doubt. Islamic law has no objections to this, as proving an offence beyond doubt is a requirement in Islamic law. *Shubhah* mentioned here exists in the mind of the accused at the time of the commission of the act on the basis of conflicting opinions about the *ḥukm* or because of a particular set of facts. An example of *shubhat al-milk* is, in the opinion of Mālik, when the offender steals (or takes by way of stealth) the property of the *bayt al-māl* (treasury) under the impression that he is part owner of the property. In law the *shubhāt* are referred to as mistakes: mistake or ignorance of fact and mistake or ignorance of law (see page 179).

3. ***Shubhah* and *ta'zīr*:** All *ta'zīr* is the right of the individual and it is for this reason that *shubhah* does not operate in it. This is the claim made by al-Kāsānī. Some jurists, mostly Shāfi'ites,[54] have said that *ta'zīr* can also be a right of Allah. This is an inconsistent statement, for *ta'zīr* as a right of Allah would prevent pardon (*'afw*), which is an acknowledged attribute of *ta'zīr*.

4. **Criminal proceedings and evidence:** The evidence of women is not admissible in the right of Allah, that is, in *ḥudūd*, while it is in the case of *ta'zīr*, which is the right of the individual, but the *niṣāb* of one man and two women has to be maintained, as in the case of other rights of the individual. No such restriction is applicable to the right of the state and a single woman can furnish evidence that is admissible in cases falling under *siyāsah*, just as circumstantial evidence is admissible whenever the *ḥaqq al-salṭanah* is in issue. In other words, the criminal proceedings and requirements of evidence change according to the right involved. In Pakistan today, *ta'zīr* and *siyāsah* are both classified under the heading of *ta'zīr*.

THIS CLASSIFICATION MAY RAISE, at least, three questions in the mind of the reader. The first question is: Are the rights of Allah and the rights of the state two different categories? The second question is: What is the difference between *ḥadd* and *ta'zīr* and why was there a need to classify offences into these two categories? The third question is: Why do the *fuqahā'* avoid the discussion of *siyāsah* jurisdiction of the *imām* and why were the *siyāsah* penalties not included in the classification of *ḥadd* or *ta'zīr*?

54. Al-Māwardī is one of the first to have said this. See *al-Aḥkām al-Sulṭānīyah*, 237. There are some later Ḥanafī jurists too who have maintained that *ta'zīr* may be a right of Allah or the right of the individual. One such Hanafī jurist is Ibn 'Ābidīn. He does, however, realize the inconsistency and is forced to say that when *ta'zīr* is a right of Allah, it cannot be commuted, that is, it will not accept *'afw* (pardon). See *Ḥāshiyat Ibn 'Ābidīn*, vol. 3, 192.

The first question arises from a confusion created by modern scholars, who have considered all public rights as the rights of Allah. What is to be realized is that even the state and the Muslim community as a whole owe rights to Allah. How then can we consider the rights of Allah and the rights of the state as one? The general rule appears to be that the rights of Allah are outside the ambit of state law: these rights cannot be altered or suspended by the state whatever the emergency. The rights of the state or public rights, on the other hand, can be suspended.

4.2.2 Why the classification into *ḥadd* and *ta'zīr*?

The second question or observation is not directly related to the first, yet the answer for both is to be found in the same place. The Federal Shariat Court of Pakistan, while hearing a petition on the question of *rajm* (stoning to death for unlawful sexual intercourse by a married person), indirectly questioned the doctrine of *ḥadd* in Islamic criminal law. The Court pointed out that the term *ḥadd* had been used on fourteen (thirteen?) different occasions in the Qur'ān, in the sense of restrictions or bounds set by Allah. None of these uses gives the meaning of *ḥadd* as a fixed penalty, which is generally the meaning assigned to the term *ḥadd* by the jurists. The Court added that it also appears from the traditions of the Prophet and the sayings of the Companions that the word *ḥadd* was used in the sense of punishment alone and not "fixed punishment." The traditions, thus, do not establish the meaning assigned to it by the *fuqahā'*. In addition to this, the jurists also differ about the number of punishments to be treated as *ḥadd*. These range from four to seventeen. On the basis of the definition of *ḥadd* given by the *fuqahā'*, all punishments awarded by the Prophet should have been treated as *ḥadd*, but the Court found it to be very strange that only a few were classified as such. The punishment of drinking of wine (*shurb al-khamr*) was not found in the Qur'ān, and was not uniform in the *Sunnah* yet, it has been treated as *ḥadd*. There is also no distinction between *ḥadd* and *ta'zīr* in the *Sunnah*. Concluding these observations, former Chief Justice of the Federal Shariat Court, Justice Aftab Hussain said: "My finding is that the word *ḥadd* has been defined by the jurists a long time after the death of the Holy Prophet."[55]

This, indeed, is an important question raised by the Court. If the concept of *ḥadd* is changed, and all punishments are classified as *ta'zīr*, or all are classified as *ḥadd*, the entire structure of criminal law as erected by the *fuqahā'* is bound to collapse and would have to be built on a different foundation. There is no difficulty in agreeing on the point that the division into *ḥadd* and *ta'zīr* is a later development, but the question as to why the *fuqahā'* treated some penalties as *ḥadd*, and not others, needs to be explained. A few points have already been explained above, but for fuller explanation we may reframe the question. Is the classification of crimes into those of *ḥadd*, *ta'zīr*, and *siyāsah* really necessary? If so, how is this classification justified?

According to modern Muslim writers the reason is that *ḥadd* punishments are fixed in the Qur'ān and *Sunnah*. This appears to be the only reason, because of which they consider punishments to be divided into two categories only: *ḥadd* and *ta'zīr*. There are, however, some problems with this, mostly of analytical consistency. This was pointed out by the Federal Shariat Court of Pakistan: Why did the *fuqahā'* choose only a few penalties out of the several awarded by the Prophet and classified them as *ḥadd*, leaving other penalties out? The answer to this question is complex, but not beyond comprehension. It may be broken up into the following points:

1. The first point is that the majority of the jurists considered those penalties as *ḥadd* that are mentioned in the Qur'ān. The penalty for drinking wine is not mentioned in the Qur'ān, but the act of drinking wine has been condemned as an offence. The penalty is found in the *Sunnah*, where it is different in different traditions, but the jurists selected a penalty according to their different methods of preferring traditions. If a difference of opinion has arisen over the extent of the penalty, it is not very important. The significant

55. *Hazoor Bakhsh vs. The State*, PLD 1983 FSC 1.

point is that the penalty has been provided by the *Sunnah*, which is an authoritative source of law.

2. The second point, and this is most important, is that all the penalties declared as *ḥadd* are governed by a certain procedure and a particular form of evidence. The Qur'ān specified four trustworthy witnesses for the offence of unlawful sexual intercourse and the *Sunnah* prescribes two for other offences. In addition, the *Sunnah* lays down different conditions for some of these offences, which must be met before punishments can be meted out. These are, for example, the conditions of *ḥirz* and *niṣāb* for the offence of *sariqah* (theft). The *ḥikmah* (wisdom) in these punishments appears to be that the primary purpose is general deterrence, even if they are applied rarely due to stringent conditions of proof. If all other punishments were also to be governed by the same rules, that is, if every punishment were to be classified as *ḥadd* and had to be proved through such high standards of evidence and proof, social control, which is the major purpose of the law, would be difficult. In addition, the evidence of women would have to be excluded from the entire criminal law. As each crime would relate to the right of Allah, forgiveness (*'afw*) and commuting of sentences, as described earlier, would also not be possible.

3. If, on the other hand, all the *ḥudūd* penalties were called *ta'zīr*, the first effect would be that the evidence of women would be included with two women replacing one man. The second difference would be that forgiveness of the sentences now called *ḥudūd* would be possible. The third effect would be that the penalties would be at the discretion of the judge or ruler, to be varied and changed as he deemed fit, when some penalties have been fixed by the Qur'ān. Further, these penalties would be declared as the right of the individual as in the case of *ta'zīr* and would no longer be associated with the concept of limits or bounds of Allah. All this would be against the teachings of the Qur'ān and the *Sunnah* of the Prophet, besides creating many logical inconsistencies.

4. Finally, the distinction flows from the rights affected. This has already been explained above.

The *fuqahā'*, then, with their knowledge of the Qur'ān and the *Sunnah* realized that the the sources of *sharī'ah* required some penalties to be maintained as the *ḥudūd* of Allah, limits or boundaries never to be crossed whatever the age or civilization and whatever the conditions of life. These were the rights of Allah.

تلك حدود الله فلا تعتدوها و من يتعد حدود الله فاولآئك هم الظالمون

> These are the limits (imposed by) Allah. Transgress them not. For whoso transgresseth Allah's limits: such are the wrongdoers.[56]

They separated these from wrongs associated with the rights of the individual. This area was called *ta'zīr*. The area of the rights of the state they left to the ruler to elaborate. These were called *siyāsah* offences. This should suffice to answer the question raised by the Federal Shariat Court.

4.2.3 Differences between *ta'zīr* and *siyāsah*

Another problem arises, however, with respect to *ta'zīr*. We have been maintaining that crimes are classified into *ḥadd* and *ta'zīr*, with *qiṣāṣ* being associated with *ḥadd*. The Islamic law of crimes as applied throughout Islamic history appears to present three categories: *ḥadd*, *ta'zīr*, and *siyāsah*. This apparent difference needs to be resolved.

The *fuqahā'* rarely discuss *ta'zīr* in detail, with the result that it is extremely difficult to determine the exact scope of *ta'zīr*. Some research has been done on this by scholars, but there is need to be more analytical and to avoid logical inconsistencies. In addition to this, the ruler carried out this function through a policy called the *siyāsah shar'īyah*. This may be translated as the "administration of justice according to the *sharī'ah*." When such administration conformed with the dictates of the *sharī'ah*, it was called *siyāsah 'ādilah*

56. Qur'ān 2 : 229

or administration according to justice. If his policy or administration deviated from the norms of *sharī'ah,* it was called *siyāsah ẓālimah* or tyrannical administration.[57]

According to the writings of the later jurists and their rulings, we can notice two main differences between *ta'zīr* and *siyāsah:*

1. *Ta'zīr* is the right of the individual, while *siyāsah* pertains to the pure right of the state. **This means that in *ta'zīr* a private injury has also been caused through the offence.** In *siyāsah* the offence is mainly against the public order. It is for this reason that habitual offenders are prosecuted under this right.

2. Accordingly, in *ta'zīr,* because it is the right of the individual, the *nisāb* of witnesses has to be maintained, ie, two female withnesses for one male witness. This is the same as in commercial transactions, because they pertain to the right of the individual. In *siyāsah* there is no such limitation and the ruler or the state may determine the standards of evidence.

Now some modern scholars conclude that *ta'zīr* can be a right of Allah and a right of the individual, and by right of Allah they mean the right of the state, because they equate the two. They base their opinion on the views of some *fuqahā'*.[58] It is, however, felt that *ta'zīr* should be designated as the right of the individual. This is the practice of the Ḥanafites and appears to be based on analytical consistency. An example will illustrate why.

> If a man steals from the *bayt al-māl* there is no *ḥadd* penalty for him. The reason is based on *shubhat al-milk.* The *bayt al-māl* is the common property of the Muslims and for purposes of *ḥadd* the offender is considered to have committed a theft from his own property that is jointly owned with the Muslims. *Ḥadd* is waived due to the doubt, actual or legal, in the mind of the offender arising from joint ownership of

57. Ṭarābalusī, *Mu'īn al-Ḥukkām* 1 (s.l, n.d.).
58. See, e.g, al-Māwardī, *al-Aḥkām al-Sulṭānīyah,* 237.

> the property. In other words, there was a mistake of law and fact. This person, however, is not allowed to go scot free. He is awarded punishment under the rights of the state, as *shubhat al-milk* is not operative against these rights, but it is effective in the waiver of punishment in the right of Allah. If *ta'zīr* is declared as a right of Allah, this particular offender will go scot free on the basis of the same *shubhah*, as the right of Allah is to be waived in such a case, which would defeat the purposes of the law and those of social control. To state it differently, if both *ḥadd* and *ta'zīr* are considered the right of Allah, the doubt or *shubhah* related to ownership would operate in both.

There is another difficulty involved with the concept of *ta'zīr*. In the case of murder or *qatl 'amd* the penalty is *qiṣāṣ*, but only when the offence is proved through the testimony of two male *'adl* witnesses. If the offence is not proved in a certain case, but there is sufficient circumstantial evidence to convict the offender, will the state try this person under *ta'zīr* or under *siyāsah*? Under *ta'zīr*, the system of the *fuqahā'* requires two witnesses again, with one male being replaced with two females, that is, almost the same kind of testimony. In *siyāsah* the standards of testimony are lowered and the case can be proved more easily.

The only solution appears to be to merge the two areas of *ta'zīr* and *siyāsah* with the standards of proof and modes of procedure being determined by the *imām*. This the Muslims appear to have done already, without taking into account the *niṣāb* for testimony.[59] The point that needs to be emphasized here is that this area, whatever the name chosen, *cannot be designated as a right of Allah*, as this would invoke *shubhah* and its consequences. In this case the right belongs to the state or to the Muslim community. This will avoid logical inconsistencies and help build upon the system erected by the *fuqahā'*.

59. Thus, for example, the *Ḥudūd* Ordinances applied in Pakistan do not require the testimony of two male witnesses. An offence classified as *ta'zīr* can be proved through the testimony of one witness, even when the witness is a female.

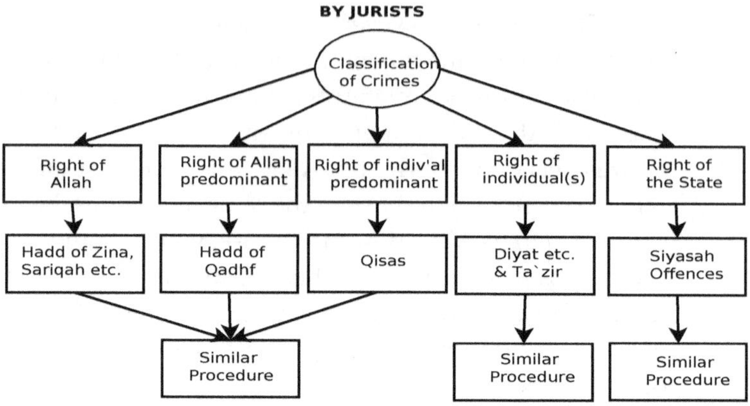

A question pertaining to commercial law may be raised here: If the *nisāb* of two female witnesses for one male witness can be eliminated in the case of *ta'zīr,* which is the right of the individual, should it not be waived in the case of other rights of the individual, ie, commercial transactions? A solution would be to interpret the Qur'ānic text as a recommendation (*nadb*) rather than as an obligation (*wujūb*).

4.3 Modern Classifications in Law

According to Cross and Jones,[60] offences may be classified according to:

1. **their source,** into statutory and common law offences. This classification does not apply to Pakistan. Even in Britain almost all common law crimes have been converted into statutory offences in conformity with the principle of legality.

2. **their effect on the law of arrest,** into arrestable and other offences.

3. **the survival of certain special rules,** into treasons and other offences. This may now be called constitutional offences and

60. Cross and Jones, *Introduction to Criminal Law,* 18–19.

other offences as the offence of treason is defined in the Constitution of Pakistan.

4. **the method by which they are tried,** into offences triable only on indictment, offences triable summarily and offences triable either way.

In Pakistan, the Criminal Procedure Code deals in great detail with the classifications at 2 and 4. The major difference is that in England, the United States and Australia trial by jury is still considered to be the best mode of determining the guilt of the accused according to the standards of the community. The Criminal Procedure Code does not provide for trial by jury.

Review Questions

① How are laws classified by the earlier British writers and what similarities do you find in such classifications with those in Islamic law?

② Provide a general classification of laws in Islam on the other basis of rights and apply this classification to the law of crimes?

③ What is the distinction between *ḥadd* and *ta'zīr,* on the one hand, and *ta'zīr* and *siyāsah* on the other?

④ Why did the Muslim jurists classify crimes into *ḥadd* and *ta'zīr*? What will be the result if this classifcation is changed?

⑤ Should *ta'zīr* and *siyāsah* offences be merged into one category? Will this affect the classification on the basis of rights?

⑥ What are the criteria on the basis of which crimes are classified in the modern world?

CHAPTER 5

PUNISHMENT AND SENTENCING

Rather let the crime of the guilty go unpunished than condemn the innocent.

Justinian I,
Law Code, A.D. 535

5.1 The Aims of Western Criminal Law

According to Sir Rupert Cross "The aim of the penal system is to reduce crime by making as many people as possible want to obey the criminal law [and] the general practice of punishment by the state is only justified if it has two objectives, the reduction of crime, and the promotion of respect for the criminal law."[61] These ideas have been incorporated in the objectives stated in the Model Penal Code drafted by the American Law Institute. Penal Codes ususally do not contain statements on objectives, however, it is to be hoped that if and when a new penal code is drafted in Pakistan (for gathering the criminal law, now spread overs a number of statutes, into one uniform document) it will clearly state the purposes of the criminal law as applied in Pakistan. A statement of the purposes of law will help in its smooth implementation as well as the evaluation of the machinery set up for its implementation.

The Americal Law Institute while framing its Model Penal Code stated the purposes of the criminal law to be the following:

> (1) The general purposes of the provisions governing the defintion of offenses are:

61. Sir Rupert Cross, *The English Sentencing System*, 3rd ed. (London: Butterworths, 1981) 121.

a) to forbid and prevent conduct that unjustifiably and inexcusably inflicts or threatens substantial harm to individual or public interests;
b) to subject to public control persons whose conduct indicates that they are disposed to commit crimes;
c) to safeguard conduct that is without fault from condemnation as criminal;
d) to give fair warning of the nature of the conduct declared to be an offense;
e) to differentiate on reasonable grounds between serious and minor offenses.

The points listed above, alongwith the general purposes governing sentencing (see section 5.3.1 at page 73) need to be studied very carefully as they incorporate the most important principles of modern criminal law.

5.2 The Aims of Islamic Criminal Law

In Islamic law the aims of punishment and sentencing are also based upon similar purposes; namely, "to forbid and prevent conduct that unjustifiably and inexcusably inflicts or threatens substantial harm to dividual or public interests." This is evident from the public and private interests that the *sharī'ah* seeks to preserve and protect. The only difference is that these are interests determined by the Lawgiver for the subjects. In the case of positive law, these interests have been determined by the people for themselves, and are likely to vary in different places and in different times. Further, the method of preference of one interest over the other, in case of conflict, is also likely to differ from the method in Islamic law. As far as respect for the Criminal law is concerned, it follows naturally from obedience to religious law.

5.2.1 The protection of interests

The interests that are required by the Lawgiver to be preserved and protected by the Islamic law are classified into five categories:

1. The preservation and protection of *Dīn*.
2. The preservation and protection of life.
3. The preservation and protection of the family.
4. The preservation and protection of the intellect.
5. The preservation and protection of wealth.

We have used the words "preservation and protection" to emphasize that these interests have a dual aspect: the affirmation and establishing of these interests and the defence of these interests.[62] The relationship of these interests with the criminal law is witnessed through the defensive aspect. Yet, it is necessary to understand the positive aspect too, because it indicates the duties of the state as well as the conditions to be created by the Muslim state for the proper functioning of the law. Some scholars may even consider the affirmation of the positive aspect a precondition for the implementation of the penalties flowing from the defensive aspect. The duties of the state emerging from the positive aspect lead us to the concept of fundamental rights in Islam.

Al-Ghazālī describes the dual feature of the *maqāṣid* through the terms *ibqā'* (affirmation; preservation) and *ḥifẓ* (protection; defence).[63] Al-Shāṭibī verifying what al-Ghazālī said about the dual aspect explains that the first aspect is "what affirms its elements and establishes its foundations," that is, of an interest determined by the Lawgiver. The second, he adds, is "what repels actual or expected disharmony."[64]

62. Those interested in knowing how these interest control all the systems and sub-systems within an Islamic state should read the author's book *Theories of Islamic Law* (Islamabad: IIIT & IRI, 1994).
63. Al-Ghazālī discusses the *maqāṣid* in his books on *uṣūl al-fiqh*, but he provides details of the affirmative aspect in *Jawāhir al-Qur'ān* (Beirut: Dār Iḥyā' al-'Ulūm, 1958) 32–35.
64. Al-Shāṭibī, *al-Muwāfaqāt*, vol. 2, 8.

Thus, from the positive aspect, it is the duty of the state to create conditions that facilitate worship and promote the establishment of the other pillars of Islam.[65] The interest of life is secured by creating conditions that promote healthy living and the welfare of human beings in general including security of life. The interest of progeny is promoted and preserved by establishing family life, which is the fundamental unit of the social system, on sound foundations.[66] The interest of intellect is preserved by providing education and securing the means for the unhindered growth of the intellect. The interest of wealth is secured by creating conditions for the growth of wealth and its equitable distribution so that it does not circulate among the wealthy alone.

From the defensive or protective aspect, interests are secured by preventing the destruction or corruption of the positive aspect. Thus, *jihād* is prescribed for defending the *Dīn*, while prayer, fasting, pilgrimage and *zakāt* help establish it. The penalties for apostasy and the blasphemy are justified on the basis of the first interest, that is, the protection of *Dīn*. Life is preserved through the provision of sustenance and the maintenance of good health, while it is protected or defended throught the provision of penalties for those who destroy life without legal justification. The penalty for murder by way of *qiṣāṣ* is based upon the interest of the protection of life. *Nasl* is promoted through the maintenance of healthy family life and the institution of marriage, while penalties are provided for those who would corrupt and destroy its values. The Islamic laws for unlawful sexual intercourse and *qadhf* defend the public and private interests in the family, which is the basic unit of the Islamic social system. The preservation of *'aql* is achieved through the provision of education and healthy conditions for its growth and advancement, while penalties are provided for the consumption of substances that destroy the intellect. The laws of prohibition (consumption of intoxicants) is based upon the protection of the intellect. Preservation of wealth is ensured through security of transactions, a primary goal of the law, while theft or misappropriation of wealth is punished.

65. Ibid. 9.
66. Ibid.

5.2.2 Priorities within interests

It should be noted that there is a definite order and priority of the interests mentioned above. *Dīn* has priority over life, therefore, a Muslim may be asked to give up his life through *jihād*. Life has priority over intellect, therefore, if a person drinks wine in a state of *iḍṭirār* (necessity) to save his life, he will not be punished. Likewise, if a persons steals food during a famine he will not be punished. Each of these interests is classified into public and individual interests and issues of law are settled through a reconciliation of the conflicting or competing interests. In each issue that comes up for decision before the judge, he will find two or more interests competing for supremacy. The competion may be between two public interests, two private interests, or between a public and a private interest. There is a complex structure of these interests and the details are to be found in the books of legal theory. Here we may point out that though the relationship of these interests is shown through *ḥudūd* and *qiṣāṣ*, the entire law of crimes in Islam has to conform with these interests whether this law falls under *ta'zīr* or *siyāsah* or some other head. The remaining purposes of the law mentioned in the Model Penal Code can also be shown to be compatible with Islamic law and some of these will be discussed in what follows.

5.3 The Nature of Punishment

We shall begin the discussion about the nature of punishment by first listing the purposes of sentencing stated in the ALI Model Penal Code as well as the essential ingredients that jurists consider punishment to have. After listing the ingredients, we shall attempt an analysis and try to identify the ingredients that Islamic law acknowledges.

5.3.1 The purposes of sentencing and the Model Penal Code

> (2) The general purposes of the provisions governing the sentencing and treatment of offenders are:

(a) to prevent the commission of offenses;
(b) to promote the correction and rehabilitation of offenders;
(c) to safeguard offenders against excessive, disproportionate or arbitrary punishment;
(d) to give fair warning of the nature of the sentences that may be imposed on conviction of an offense;
(e) to differentiate among offenders with a view to a just individualization in their treatment;
(f) to define coordinate and harmonize the powers, duties and functions of the courts and of administrative officers and agencies responsible for dealing with offenders;
(g) to advance the use of generally accepted scientific methods and knowledge in sentencing and treatment of offenders;
(h) to integrate responsibility for the administration of the correctional system in a State Department....

Islamic law would in general agree with most purposes of sentencing. There may be some discussion about the purposes at (c) above, however, as we indicate below. Some of the purposes are determined by human reason, while others are handed down by the Lawgiver and are to be accepted as they are. The response, then, would be that Islamic law does not consider certain punishments to be excessive or disproportionate, especially when they are viewed in the light of the philosophy behind their implementation.

5.3.2 The essential ingredients of punishment

Delineating cases that are not fit for punishment, Jeremy Bentham says:

§1. General view of cases unmeet for punishment

> I. The general object which all laws have, or ought to have, in common, is to augment the total happiness of the community; and therefore, in the first place, to exclude, as far as may be, every thing that tends to subtract from that happiness: in other words, to exclude mischief.
>
> II. But all punishment is mischief: all punishment in itself is evil. Upon the principle of utility, if it ought at all to be admitted, it ought only to be admitted in as far as it promises to exclude some greater evil.
>
> III. It is plain, therefore, that in the following cases punishment ought not to be inflicted.
>
> 1. Where it is *groundless*: where there is no mischief for it to prevent; the act not being mischievous upon the whole.
> 2. Where it must be *inefficacious*: where it cannot act so as to prevent the mischief.
> 3. Where it is *unprofitable,* or too *expensive:* where the mischief it would produce would be greater than what it prevented.
> 4. Where it is *needless:* where the mischief may be prevented, or cease of itself, without it: that is, at a cheaper rate.[67]

The points mentioned by Bentham are to be examined in the light of the meaning of *maṣlaḥah* as compared to the principle of utility. The distinction lies in the fact that pure utility is based on human reason, while *maṣlaḥah* is based on what the Lawgiver deems beneficial.

5.3.3 Analysis of the ingredients of punishment

It is well known that the criminal law owes much to Jeremy Bentham, who has had a great influence on the development of mod-

67. Jeremy Bentham, *An Introduction to the Principles of Morals and Legislation* (1907 (First published 1789)) 170–71.

ern criminal law, especially in Britain. Even the ranges of penalties (upto 10 years and so on) are the result of his efforts at reform. The philosophy working behind his statements is based on the well known principle of utility. This principle upholds a single moral law for all lawmaking: "The greatest happiness of the greatest number." All punishment, according to this principle, must be inflicted if it promotes the happiness of the community. If punishment is bringing more misery to the community than happiness, then, it is to be thrown out.

ISLAMIC LAW, in general, upholds the ideas about punishment put forward by Jeremy Bentham, but there are a few vital differences that must be understood.

The principle in Islamic law that corresponds to Bentham's principle of utility is called *maṣlaḥah.* Some writers have found so many similarities between the two methods that they have equated the two. *Maṣlaḥah,* like utility, means the acquisition of *manfa'ah* (utility) and the repelling of *maḍarrah* (harm). This, however, is the literal meaning and not the technical legal meaning of the principle. Al-Ghazālī defines the principle to indicate how it differs from the modern principle of utility. He says:

> As for *maslaḥah,* it is essentially an expression for the acquisition of *manfa'ah* (benefit) or the repulsion of *maḍarrah* (injury, harm), but that is not what we mean by it, because acquisition of *manfa'ah* and the repulsion of *maḍarrah* represent human goals, that is, the welfare of humans through the attainment of these goals. What we mean by *maṣlaḥah,* however, is *the preservation of the ends of the shar'.*[68]

This brings out the important difference between the principle of utility and the Islamic principle of *maṣlaḥah* that in Islam what leads to utility is determined by the Lawgiver and not by human desires. Thus, the difference with reference to penalties and punishments may be summed in a simple statement: Punishments that may not appeal to the human mind are still legally binding in the Islamic state as they promote human welfare in the eyes of the Lawgiver.

68. Al-Ghazālī, *al-Mustaṣfā min 'Ilm al-Uṣūl,* Baghdad, 1294 (A.H.), i, 286.

5.3.4 Types of punishments: Western and Islamic

The usual punishments awarded after criminal proceedings under Western legal systems are: imprisonment and fines. In the Islamic criminal justice system, the various penalties may be stated in terms of the rights involved:

1. **Where the right of Allah is involved—either completely or in part—*ḥudūd* and *qiṣāṣ*:**
2. **Where the right of the individual alone is involved—*ta'zīr*, reparation and compensation as substituted penalty after *sulḥ*:**
3. **Where the right of the state is involved including *fasād fi'l-arḍ***

§53 of the Pakistan Penal Code lists the following punishments:

The punishments to which offenders are liable under the provisions of this Code are:—

Firstly,	*Qiṣāṣ;*
Secondly,	*Diyat;*
Thirdly,	*Arsh;*
Fourthly,	*Ḍamān;*
Fifthly,	*Ta'zīr;*
Sixthly,	Death;
Seventhly,	Imprisonment for life;
Eighthly,	Imprisonment which is of two descriptions, namely:— (i) Rigorous *i.e.,* with hard labour; (ii) Simple;
Ninthly,	Forfeiture of property;
Tenthly,	Fine.

5.3.5 Is imprisonment the preferred penalty in Islam?

Imprisonment is the preferred form of punishment in the modern world. The offender is separated from society so that he can no longer cause harm. During his stay in prison, efforts may be made for his rehabilitation. Nevertheless, there are many critics too. These critics advance a large number of arguments, foremost among them being that prisons have become schools for the production of hardened criminals. Another, reason advanced is that maintaining prisons today is becoming increasingly expensive and the tax payer may not be able to bear this burden. Chief Justice Burger of the US Supreme Court advocated that prisons should be converted into "factories with fences."

Here we are not interested in advancing arguments for and against imprisonment. Our purpose is to examine the status accorded to this form of punishment by Islamic law.

The majority of the jurists agree relying on evidences in the Qur'ān, the *Sunnah* and consensus of opinion that imprisonment (*ḥabs*) is a valid form of punishment. There is, however, a problem when we come to determining the duration of imprisonment. The Ḥanafī jurists maintain that the matter of duration is to be left to the state to determine, and their is no fixed duration. The duration, they say, varies with the nature of the crime and the record of the offender. The Ḥanbalīs say the same thing: the duration is to fit the crime. According to the Shāfi'īs, the duration of imprisonment should under no circumstances reach one year. Some of them say that is should be two months, while others restrict it to six months. Al-Māwardī, however, has related some conflicting opinions on the issue. The Mālikīs maintain that it should range between two months and six months.

What is the rule here? It is well known that the earlier jurists tried to base their opinion on some evidence from the texts. The evidence for those who do not permit imprisonment of more than a year is a tradition that determines the *ḥadd* of unlawful sexual intercourse by an unmarried person to be 100 stripes *plus* exile for a year. Exile may be converted into imprisonment. As *ta'zīr* in no case is to exceed the maximum *ḥadd*, imprisonment cannot exceed one year as this is the maximum reported *ḥadd*..

Those who do not fix a duration for imprisonment maintain that one year's exile given in addition to *ḥadd* as stripes is not part of the *ḥadd*. It is *ta'zīr,* which may be awarded at the discretion of the ruler. For considering it *ta'zīr,* they rely on precedents from the early *khulafā',* who awarded the penalty sometimes and waived it on other occasions, which shows that it must have been a discretionary penalty.

Even if it is accepted that imprisonment as a form of punishment should be used sparingly, the issue would be: what penalty are we to use instead?

REVIEW QUESTIONS

① Compare the aims of criminal law in Islam with those in positivist systems?

② List the rules of punishment in the light of a comparison between the principles of utility and *maṣlaḥah.*

③ "Respect for the law is the only aim of criminal law." Comment.

④ On what basis would you justify Islamic punisments considered brutal according to Western standards?

⑤ Classify punishments in Islam on the basis of the underlying rights.

⑥ What is the Islamic view on imprisonment as the preferred form of punishment?

CHAPTER 6

THEORIES OF PUNISHMENT

> *As one reads history, not in the expurgated editions written for schoolboys and passmen, but in the original authorities of each time, one is absolutely sickened, not by the crimes that the wicked have committed, but by the punishments that the good have inflicted; and a community is infinitely more brutalised by the habitual employment of punishment than it is by the occasional occurrence of crime.*
>
> Oscar Wilde,
> *The Soul of Man Under Socialism*

A discussion of the theories of law flows out naturally from a consideration of the aims of criminal law discussed in the previous chapter. We have separated the two topics only for ease of study; otherwise the two topic should be taken up together.

We take up the discussion of the theories of punishment with a quotation from Sir Rupert Cross, who doubts the very utility of discussing these theories as "theories." He says:

> In many ways it is a pity that the word "theories" ever came to be employed to describe the moral justifications of the practice of punishing with various degrees of severity .... As punishment by definition entails the deliberate infliction of pain, it certainly needs to be justified morally, but the use of the word "theory" is unfortunate for at least two reasons. In the first place, it suggests that one theory must be right to the exclusion of all others whereas, [ ] it may well be the case that neither retributive theories standing alone nor utilitarian theories standing alone can provide an adequate answer to any of the major questions that are commonly raised

> with regard to punishment. The second objection to the use of the expression "theories of punishment" is that it tends to produce interminable and unconclusive discussions concerning the correctness of any one of them."[69]

Nevertheless, theories of punishment are formulated by jurists to answer some fundamental questions: Is the aim of punishment simply to mete out an appropriate punishment to a wrongdoer? Is it intended to deter the wrongdoer as well as others from committing such offences in the future? Is it intended to protect the public by shutting the offender away? Does punishment reform the offender? Are all of these objectives intended by the criminal law? After answering all these questions we face another important question: What measure is most appropriate to achieve the desired objective? In other words, what quantum of punishment is suitable for each offender. [70]

Theories of punishment go under different names: theory of retribution; theory of deterrence; theory of reformation; and theory of prevention and rehabilitation. In general, theories that uphold the reduction of crime as the aim of the criminal law are described as "utilitarian" theories, while those that require that the offenders be given their deserts (what they rightfully deserve) are described as "retributive."[71] According to such a classification deterrence, reform and prevention are included in utilitarian theories. For ease of description and analysis, we shall consider each theory independently, and the first theory we take up is that of retribution.

6.1 The Theory of Retribution

Of all the theories advanced by jurists and philosophers, it is the theory or retribution that has attracted the greatest attention. The

69. Cross, *The English sentencing System*, 120-21.
70. Smith and Hogan, *Criminal Law*, 4. Rupert Cross maintains that the main questions are: Why punish? Who should be punished? How much punishment should be inflicted? Cross *The English Sentencing System*, 121.
71. Cross, *The English Sentencing System*, 128.

reason is that the justification of punishment according to this theory is based on the natural reaction of man. The theory may be said to be based upon the words of the Exalted, "O ye who believe! The law of equality is prescribed to you in cases of murder: the free for the free, the slave for the slave, the woman for the woman."[72] Surprisingly, Muslim jurists uphold deterrence even in cases of *qiṣāṣ*, as we shall explain below.

6.1.1 Moral blameworthiness

The basic assumption of the retributive theory is that a crime is essentially a moral wrong. The well known doctrine of *mens rea* is also based upon this idea, because it requires a blameworthy intention. A morally blameworthy act is also equated with sin, and the idea of moral blameworthiness itself is based upon the power of human beings to choose between right and wrong. A person committing an evil act is to be held responsible for the consequences.[73]

The law also assumes that the evil resulting from an act can be measured and graded and this enables us to award punishments in accordance with the gravity of the offence (an eye for an eye and a tooth for a tooth). In practice, however, this gradation varies from fines to life imprisonment to death. In this system of gradation, it is realized that some offences may be so minor that they do not deserve a punishment. The framers of law, therefore, fix a maximum punishment, but there is usually no minimum. The awarding of the right penalty within this range is left to the discretion of the judge. Murder is an exception to this rule of discretion. Many of the maximum penalties, it is maintained, were fixed in the nineteenth century and there may be a need to revise or reconsider these. When the penalties fixed are absolutely out of proportion with the gravity of the offence, the range provided to the judge fails to serve as a guide. (See the purposes of punishment at page 73)

72. Qur'ān 2 : 178.
73. Smith and Hogan, *Criminal Law*, 4.

The meaning of moral blameworthiness and a retributive penalty for it may be stated in the words of Stephen:

> I am ...of opinion that this close alliance between criminal law and moral sentiment is in all ways healthy and advantageous to the community. I think it highly desirable that criminals should be hated, that the punishments inflicted upon them should be so contrived as to give expression to that hatred, and to justify it so far as the provision of means for expressing and gratifying a healthy and natural sentiment can justify and encourage it.[74]

The views of judges and jurists are much more lenient as compared to this strict view. Muslim jurists highlight the moral blameworthiness of certain serious offences and show that the Islamic law takes this aspect into account. For example al-Sarakhsī, the great Ḥanafī jurist, talking about murder and *qiṣāṣ* says:

> For the gravity of the offence in murder (*qatl al-'amd*) our scholars (Ḥanafīs) did not uphold expiation (*kaffārah*) for the murderer, because the threat is explicitly stated in the texts and cannot be alleviated with expiation. The sin in it is too grave to be atoned through expiation. Further, it is the same whether *qiṣāṣ* has become obligatory in it or not, as in the case of a father killing his son ....[75]

Giving the background of the issue he adds:

> The crime (*jināyah*) against life has as its ultimate what is committed with pure malice, and this is greatest of all prohibited things after polytheism (*shirk*). Allāh, the Exalted, has said:
>
> مِن أَجلِ ذٰلِكَ كَتَبنَا عَلَى بَنِى إِسرَآئِيلَ أَنَّهُ مَن قَتَلَ نَفساً بِغَيرِ نَفسٍ أَو فَسَاداً فِى الأَرضِ فَكَأَنَّمَا قَتَلَ النَّاسَ جَمِيعاً
>
> "On that account: We ordained for the children of Israel that if anyone slew a person—unless it be [in retaliation]

74. James Fitzgerald Stephen, *A History of Criminal Law of England* (1883) vol. 1, 81–82.
75. Al-Sarakhsī, *Al-Mabsūṭ*, vol. 27, 84.

> for murder or for spreading mischief in the land—it would be as if he slew the whole people." [Qur'ān 5 : 32]
>
> Thus, He deemed the taking of one life as the destruction of the whole world—if only this had been in the power of human beings. He deemed it so, because an individual stands in the place of a group in the invitation to the *dīn* and in cooperation with all those who cooperate with him—cooperation among the people being obvious. Therefore, he who kills an individual severs this benefit. This is supported by the saying of the Messenger, on him be peace and blessings, that "the end of the world is acceptable to Allāh more easily than the killing of a Muslim," as well as his saying that "to think badly of a believer is disobedience (*fisq*) and fighting him is *kufr*," even though fighting here refers to fighting due to his faith, yet the apparent meaning indicates the gravity of the offence of killing a Muslim.
>
> It is for this reason that Ibn 'Abbās, may Allāh be pleased with them both, did not uphold the [effectiveness] of the repentance of a murderer. His opinion was not accepted until it was related that a person asked him saying "What do you say about [the verse] 'If a man kills a believer'? He said, 'His recompense is Hell, to abide therein (for ever): and the wrath and curse of Allāh are upon him, and a dreadful penalty is prepared for him.' He said to him, 'Except for one who repents, does good deeds, and then receives right guidance?' He (Ibn 'Abbās) replied, 'From where will guidance come to him. I heard the Messenger of Allāh (p.b.u.h.) saying that one who has killed intentionally will be brought to the Throne of al-Raḥmān on the day of judgement alongwith the slain victim, who will say, 'Ask this person why he killed me?' And, it is for this case that the verse 'If a man kills a believer....' has been revealed, and it has not been abrogated by any other [evidence] from your Prophet."[76]

This shows that Islamic law accords importance to the moral blameworthiness of the act. It is for this reason that for the offence of murder (*'amd*) the Ḥanafīs do not permit the acceptance of *kaffārah* for atonement and the repentance of the killer goes invain.[77]

76. Ibid.
77. Some of the other schools have a different opinion on this point.

6.1.2 Proportionality to guilt

The judges who still maintain this theory insist that punishment should be proportioned according to guilt. If the task of the judge is justice, then, the only way the judge can award the right punishment is by asking whether or not the offender deserved this punishment. Such judges say that if the concept of deserved punishment is eliminated, the concept of justice would be eliminated with it too.

The main question that is faced by jurists having such an approach is: By what standard should the judges estimate the punishment to be awarded to the offender? The answer to this question is provided by Denning LJ:

> The punishment inflicted for grave crimes should adequately reflect the revulsion felt by the great majority of citizens for them. It is a mistake to consider the objects of punishment as being deterrent or reformative or preventive and nothing else ...The ultimate justification of any punishment is not that it is a deterrent, but that it is the emphatic denunciation by the community of a crime....

This question of proportionality to guilt or that the offender must get what he deserves has occupied the minds of many thinkers, and the theory of retribution on the basis of proportionality has been upheld by philosophers like Kant and Hegel among others. Immanuel Kant said:

> What kind and what degree of punishment does public legal justice adopt as its principle and standard? None other than the principle of equality (illustrated by the pointer on the scales of justice), that is, the principle of not treating one side more favorably than the other. Accordingly, any undeserved evil that you inflict on someone else among the people is one that you do to yourself. If you vilify him, you vilify yourself; if you steal from him, you steal from yourself; if you kill him, you kill yourself. Only the Law of retribution (*jus talionis*) can determine exactly the kind and degree of punishment; it must be well understood, however, that this determination [must be made] in the chambers of a court of justice (and not in your private judgment). All other stan-

> dards fluctuate back and forth and, because extraneous considerations are mixed with them, they cannot be compatible with the principle of pure and strict legal justice.[78]

Hegel said:

> [W]hat is involved in the action of the criminal is not only the concept of crime, the rational aspect present in crime as such whether the individual wills it or not, the aspect which the state has to vindicate, but also the abstract rationality of the individual's *volition*. Since that is so, punishment is regarded as containing the criminal's right and hence by being punished he is honoured as a rational being. He does not receive this due of honour unless the concept and measure of his punishment are derived from his own act. Still less does he receive it if he is treated either as a harmful animal who has to be made harmless, or with a view to deterring and reforming him.[79]

Oliver Wendell Holmes, the famous American Judge, commenting upon the ideas of Hegel said:

> [T]here is a mystic bond between wrong and punishment ...Hegel...puts it, in his quasi-mathematical form, that wrong being the negation of right, punishment is the negation of that negation, or retribution. Thus the punishment must be equal, in the sense of proportionate to the crime, because its only function is to destroy it. Others, without this logical apparatus, are content to rely upon a felt necessity that suffering should follow wrongdoing.[80]

The theory is by no means dead, and there are many judges who still maintain the soundness of this theory. Some critics, however, argue that the theory is a relic of barbarism, but judges in the Western world disagree with this criticism. The debate has been going on for centuries. J. S. Mill recognized this very early. He said:

---

78. Immanuel Khant, *The Metaphysical Elements of Justice,* Trans. J. Ladd (U.S.A.: Bobbs-Merril) 100–101 (First published (in German) in 1797).
79. Hegel, *Philosophy of Right,* trans. K Knox (1942), 71.
80. Oliver Wendell Holmes, *The Common Law* (M. Howe ed. 1963), 42.

> No rule on the subject [of "the proper apportionment of punishments to offences"] recommends itself so strongly to the primitive and spontaneous sentiment of justice, as the *lex talionis*, an eye for an eye and a tooth for a tooth. Though this principle of the Jewish and of the Mahomedan law has been generally abandoned in Europe as a practical maxim, there is, I suspect, in most minds, a secret hankering after it; and when retribution accidentally falls on an offender in that precise shape, the general feeling of satisfaction evinced bears witness how natural is the sentiment to which this repayment in kind is acceptable.[81]

Al-Sarakhsī highlights this meaning too in the light of the offence of murder in the *Kitāb al-Diyāt* as follows:

> *Qiṣāṣ* expresses the meaning of equality (المساواة). In its primary usage it means following in the tracks [of someone]. Allāh, the Exalted says: وَ قَالَت لِأُختِه قُصِّيه "And she said to the sister of (Moses), 'Follow him.'"[82] Following in the tracks of someone (or something) amounts to doing exactly the same thing. It is, therefore, deemed an expression of equality.[83]

He acknowledges the background of this idea of proportionalty and elaborates its meaning for us:[84]

> *Qiṣāṣ* is established by the words of the Exalted:
>
> وَ كَتَبنَا عَلَيهِم فِيهَآ أَنَّ النَّفسَ بِالنَّفسِ وَالعَينَ بِالعَينِ وَالأَنفَ بِالأَنفِ وَالأُذُنَ بِالأُذُنِ وَالسِّنَّ بِالسِّنِّ وَالجُرُوحَ قِصَاصٌ
>
> "We ordained therein for them: 'Life for life, eye for eye, nose for nose, ear for ear, tooth for tooth, and wounds equal for equal."[85] What Allāh, the Exalted, has communicated here is that He ordained it for those

81. See J.S. Mill, *Utilitarianism* (Everyman Am. ed., 1951).
82. Qur'ān 28 : 11.
83. Al-Sarakhsī, *Al-Mabsūṭ*, vol. 26, 60.
84. Ibid.
85. Qur'ān 5 : 45.

before us and it is ordained for us too as long as there is no evidence abrogating it. He laid down that it is ordained for us, saying:

يَٰٓأَيُّهَا ٱلَّذِينَ ءَامَنُوا۟ كُتِبَ عَلَيْكُمُ ٱلْقِصَاصُ فِى ٱلْقَتْلَى ۖ ٱلْحُرُّ بِٱلْحُرِّ وَٱلْعَبْدُ بِٱلْعَبْدِ وَٱلْأُنثَىٰ بِٱلْأُنثَىٰ ۚ فَمَنْ عُفِىَ لَهُۥ مِنْ أَخِيهِ شَىْءٌ فَٱتِّبَاعٌۢ بِٱلْمَعْرُوفِ وَأَدَآءٌ إِلَيْهِ بِإِحْسَٰنٍ ۗ ذَٰلِكَ تَخْفِيفٌ مِّن رَّبِّكُمْ وَرَحْمَةٌ ۗ فَمَنِ ٱعْتَدَىٰ بَعْدَ ذَٰلِكَ فَلَهُۥ عَذَابٌ أَلِيمٌ ﴿٢:١٧٨﴾

"O ye who believe! The law of equality is prescribed for you in case of murder: the free for the free, the slave for the slave, the woman for the woman. But if any remission is made by the brother of the slain, then grant any reasonable demand and compensate him with handsome gratitude; this is a concession and a mercy from your Lord. After this whoever exceeds the limits shall be in grave penalty."[86]

There are, however, problems with the idea of proportionality, and Rupert Cross discusses one such issue. He says, "Punishment may also be undeserved if it is imposed despite the absence of fault on the defendant's part. English law contains a number of offences of 'strict liability' for which no fault is required."[87] The law of Pakistan, we may add, also contains offences of strict liability, and so does Islamic law. We shall be discussing this issue under the heading of strict liability. This objection applies to the point of moral blameworthiness too.

6.1.2.1 Desire for vengeance.

The idea of proportioning the punishment to the public's view of moral culpability is closely associated with another idea. This

86. Qur'ān 2 : 178.
87. Cross, *The English Sentencing System*, 126.

idea is of the necessity of satisfying the public desire for vengeance against the wrongdoer. Beneath this idea is the concept of retaliation that a crime arouses.[88]

Modern criminologists, on the other hand, have for some time looked down upon the retributive approach. They considered this approach barbarous. In recent times, we find a return to retribution in the criminal law. The basic reason for this is the failure to arrive at the proper method of reforming criminals. In fact, it is generally believed that prisons have become training schools for criminals, where first time offenders are turned into callous and hardened criminals. Further, preventive punishments are considered unfair and oppressive.[89]

Al-Saraksī mentions this element of retribution too in the provision of the penalty of *qiṣāṣ*. He says: "The law has made *qiṣāṣ* obligatory by way of vengeance and the cleansing of the breast of the *walī* and the rage that he can give vent to."[90]

6.1.2.2 The harm done

Retribution has another aspect to it, in addition to those described above, and this is that punishment should be awarded in proportion to the harm done. This is visible in the awarding of punishments for attempted crimes. The moral guilt of the person who attempts a crime and is successful is the same as the person who attempts the crime and fails. Yet, the punishment awarded for attempt alone is lesser than that awarded for the completed crime. Failure in the commission of the crime is considered as a mitigating factor. In such cases, it appears that punishment is being proportioned to the harm done, because a person who attempts a crime and fails has caused less harm as compared to one who has succeeded.[91]

Jurists believe that a "crude retaliation theory" is at work in this approach. The basis for such criticism is that the judge (or

88. Smith and Hogan, *Criminal Law*, 7.
89. Ibid.
90. Al-Sarakhsī, *al-Mabsūṭ*, vol. 26, 61.
91. Smith and Hogan, *Criminal Law*, 8.

the legislator who prescribes the penalty) is awarding a greater punishment for a consummated crime in order to satisfy public opinion, which is ready to tolerate a severe sentence for the consummated crime rather than an attempt.[92]

From the Islamic point of view, the idea that the punishment should be in proportion to the harm done perfected through reparations, which Western law has abolished. Islamic law provides it in the shape of *diyah, ḍamān, arsh* and so on.

6.1.2.3 The sentence to fit the crime

There are those who raise the questions as to whether there is a "normal" sentence for an offence? In response, there is general agreement that while there is no normal sentence for an offence, there certainly is a "tariff" or range within which the normal sentence is to be found. This normal varies according to the circumstances of the case and the character of the accused. Many believe that this normal within the range can only be explained in terms of the proportionality of the sentence to the circumstances of the case and subtraction from the right sentence due to mitigating circumstances. These ideas too are based on the theory of retribution.[93]

6.1.2.4 Justice and equality

Treating the offenders equally when they have an equal degree of moral guilt is considered a fundamental rule of justice. On the basis of this idea it is the endeavour of a judge to impose the penalty that has been imposed by other judges under similar circumstances. This rule is also based upon the idea of proportionality to guilt and the law does not allow anyone to be made a scapegoat in order to satisfy the whims of the public at the moment judgement is passed.[94] The theory of deterrence, on the other hand, is based on this idea in certain cases, as will be discussed below.

92. Ibid.
93. Ibid.
94. Ibid.

6.2 Deterrence or the Protection of the Public

The prime object of the criminal law, according to some, is the protection of the public by the reduction of crime and the maintenance of law and order. The prominent judicial view is that this object is attained by deterrence.

6.2.1 Primary and secondary deterrence

Deterrence is of two types: primary deterrence and secondary deterrence also referred to as individual deterrence and general deterrence.[95] Primary deterrence is for the offender himself, while secondary deterrence is intended to deter others from committing the same crime. The idea common to the deterrent theories of punishment is that the experience, threat or example of punishment discourages crime.[96]

The idea of primary deterrence is that the offender should be given such an unpleasant time that, through fear of punishment, he will never repeat his conduct.[97] In general deterrence the aim of punishment is to discourage others, who are prone to commit crime, by the threat of punishment and the example of the punishment of the offender. According to Jeremy Bentham, general deterrence was the primary aim of punishment and the writings of others like Beccaria also indicate the same.

This approach may be in conflict with the view discussed above that sentences should be proportionate to one another.[98] Judge Asquith LJ illustrated this point as follows:

> Everyone has heard of an "exemplary" sentence: and nearly everyone agrees that at times such sentences are justified. But it is not always observed that an exemplary sentence is unjust; and unjust to the precise extent that it is exemplary. Assume a particular crime is becoming dangerously

95. Cross, *The English Sentencing System,* 135–43. Cross also discusses the ideas of short-term and long term deterrence. Ibid. 38.
96. Ibid. 135.
97. Ibid.
98. Smith and Hogan, *Criminal Law,* 12.

> frequent. In normal times the appropriate sentence would be, say, two years. The judge awards three; he awards the third year entirely to deter others. This may be expedient; it may even be imperative. But one thing it is not; it is not just. The guilt of the man who commits a crime when it happens to be on the increase is no greater than that of another man who commits the same crime when it is on the wane. The truth is that in such cases the judge is not administering strict justice but choosing the lesser of two practical evils. He decides that a moderate injustice to the criminal is a lesser evil than the consequences to the public of a further rise in the crime-wave.[99]

As compared to this Salmon J expressing his views extra-judicially said:

> Nothing is more effective to stamp out crime than a long term of imprisonment. That may sound harsh, but we have to remember the twelve thousand or so of ordinary people who last year were the victims of crimes of violence. They, and their like, must be protected. *And in these circumstances it does not wring my withers at all to be told how awful it is that a comparatively young man should be shut up for a long time.*[100]

There is another aspect of the theory highlighted by Cross under the title of long-term detterence. He maintains that the views discussed so far pertain to theories of short-term deterrence that may force the offender to say, "I had better not do it because, if I am caught, I will get what I got before or worse." A person who has not committed a crime so far, but who is contemplating one, may say, "I had better not do it because, if I am caught, I will get what old—got." As compared to these short-term theories, the long-term view maintains that deterrence helps societies to build up or maintain people's standards. Thus, over a period of time people may not abstain from the crime due to fear, but due their

99. *The Listener,* XLIII at 821 as quoted in Smith and Hogan, *Criminal Law,* 13.
100. R.M. Jackson, *Enforcing the Law,* 209 as quoted in Smith and Hogan, *Criminal Law,* 13 (emphasis added).

inner feeling about its wickedness. Cross attributes these ideas to Sir James Stephen and to Dr. A. C. Ewing.[101]

Even the long-term view it is said does not justify using one individual by awarding him excessive punishment in order to maintain people's standards or to educate them.[102]

These views show that like the principles of justice, other ethical considerations are put aside in the interests of protecting the public. For this reason some judges maintain that this theory conflicts with the principle that a human being must be treated as an end in himself and not as a means to the benefiting of other persons, but they acknowledge at the same time that the theory provides a practical justification for punishment that few persons of common sense would, on reflection, reject.[103]

When courts speak of protecting society through deterrence, they are generally speaking of secondary deterrence, that is, the deterrence of others and not the deterrence of the offender. Society, however, may also be protected by locking up the individual offender for a long period, but this again brings us up against the principle of the just punishment. It is for this reason that judges are reluctant to increase punishment beyond what is deserved merely for the protection of the public from a particular offender. When the offender has a blameless record the courts do award a lesser punishment as compared to the offender who has a bad record even though this does imply that an offender is being punished for his past crimes.[104]

The general rule is that even where the sentence imposed is for the protection of the public, it should not exceed the maximum merited by the gravity of the offence. In England, the courts have departed from this principle in order to protect the public from a dangerous offender.[105]

101. Cross, *The English Sentencing System,* 138–39.
102. Ibid. 140.
103. Smith and Hogan, *Criminal Law,* 13.
104. Ibid.
105. Ibid.

6.2.2 Deterrence and Islamic law

In Islamic law, the idea of deterrence is supported by most of the prescribed penalties. Even the penalty of *qiṣāṣ*, which does have some attributes of retribution in it as shown above, is primarily meant for deterrence. The purpose of the penalty of *qiṣāṣ*, according to al-Sarakhsī, is deterrence as well as retribution. About deterrence he says: "Had the deterrence in the threat been confined to the Hereafter, only a few would have been deterred, because the majority of the people are deterred by the fear of immediate punishment that is destructive for the offender or is ruinous for him. Thus, Allāh ordained *qiṣāṣ* as well as *diyah* for the realization of the meaning of deterrence." Explaining the wisdom behind this, he says:

> *Qiṣāṣ* is established by the words of the Exalted, "We ordained therein for them: 'Life for life, eye for eye, nose for nose, ear for ear, tooth for tooth, and wounds equal for equal.'[106] What Allāh, the Exalted, has communicated here is that He ordained it for those before us and it is ordained for us too as long as there is no evidence abrogating it. He laid down that it is ordained for us, saying, "O ye who believe! The law of equality is prescribed for you in case of murder: the free for the free, the slave for the slave, the woman for the woman. But if any remission is made by the brother of the slain, then grant any reasonable demand and compensate him with handsome gratitude; this is a concession and a mercy from your Lord. After this whoever exceeds the limits shall be in grave penalty."[107] Thereafter, He elaborated the *ḥikmah* (wisdom) behind it by His words, ﴿ وَلَكُمْ فِي ٱلْقِصَاصِ حَيَوٰةٌ يَـٰٓأُو۟لِى ٱلْأَلْبَـٰبِ لَعَلَّكُمْ تَتَّقُونَ ﴾ ٢:١٧٩ "In the law of equality there is (saving) of life for you, O ye men of understanding! That ye may restrain yourselves.[108] In this there are two meanings. First, that there is life in it by way of deterrence, because a person who intends to kill his enemy feels deterred when he contemplates that if he kills him he shall be killed in return. This results in life for both

106. Qur'ān 5 : 45
107. Qur'ān 2 : 178
108. Qur'ān 2 : 179.

> of them. Second, there is life in it by way of repelling the cause of destruction, because one who kills without justification becomes a threat for the *awliyā'* of the victim out of fear of death at their hands. He, therefore, intends to destroy them for the eradication of this fear. The law, for this reason, enables them to slay him by way of *qiṣāṣ* and remove the evil threatening them. This results in the saving of life of those living."[109]

Here al-Saraskhsī is talking about secondary deterrence, that is, for those contemplating murder—the would-be murderers. Primary deterrence is not relevant here, because the offender subject to *qiṣāṣ* for murder will exist no more. Primary deterrence is relevant, however, in the case of *qiṣāṣ* for bodily injuries.[110]

One of the major purposes of law stated at the beginning of this chapter was the prevention of harm or threats to the interests preserved and protected by the *sharī'ah*. The deterrent quality of *qiṣāṣ* and the *ḥudūd* penalties ensures such preservation and protection. In the preservation of these interests, we may add, is manifest the meaning of long-term deterrence as well through which the standards of the people as required by the *sharī'ah* are maintained. The relationship of *qiṣāṣ* with the prevention of harm to the interest in life is described by al-Sarakhsī above when he points to the words of the Lawgiver, "In the law of equality there is (saving) of life for you, O ye men of understanding! That ye may restrain yourselves."[111]

Strict Islamic law does not permit the awarding of excessive penalty to an individual for the sake of deterring others. Some Muslim jurists, however, grant this right to the ruler under *ta'zīr* or under *siyāsah*. Thus, in the case of a habitual offender who has committed murder, they grant the right to the ruler to punish him even after the heirs have agreed to forgive him with or without payment of compensation.

---

109. Al-Sarakhsī, *al-Mabsūṭ*, vol. 26, 60.
110. The explanation given by al-Sarakhsī also contains a hint about the prevention of kin revenge that was prevalent in the early days.
111. Qur'ān 2 : 179

6.3 The Theory of Reformation and Rehabilitation

In modern times, a substantial part of the legislation is directed toward the rehabilitation of the offender. This is one of the main purposes of punishment stated earlier (see page 73). A large number of writers also maintain that reformation should be the main, if not the only, object of sentencing, but there are those who oppose this view. Thus, Lord Goddard CJ is reported to have said that:

> The function of the criminal law is deterrence, not reform. As law, it was not concerned with the reform of the criminal. That was a matter for those persons and societies who, to their honour, were trying to do something about it.[112]

J. Mabbot had the following to say about sentiments of reform:

> It is often thought that...the reform theory, is modern and humane compared with the retributive theory, which is primitive and barbaric. But the essential point about retributive punishment is that it treats the criminal as a man. A law is not, as the determinists would hold, a particular kind of cause (on a level with a drug or hypnosis or psychiatric treatment). It is not a cause at all, because it presents a choice and assumes freedom and responsibility. Retribution is the agent's own act. The law can *threaten*, but there is only one thing that can justify a punishment and that is something the legislator cannot bring about, namely, a free choice by the subject.... To be punished for reform reasons is to be treated like a dog. A sane adult demands to be held responsible for his actions. He rejects as an intolerable insult the well-meaning exculpations of the sympathetic scientist, whether presented on social or psychological grounds. Retributive punishment closes the account, reformative punishment opens it.[113]

---

112. (1958) 122 JPN at 479 as quoted in Smith and Hogan, *Criminal Law*, 15.
113. J. Mabbot, "Freewill and Punishment," *Contemporary British Philosophy* (H. Lewis ed., 1956), 289, 303.

From the opinions of judges and writers, it can be concluded that whenever there is a conflict between deterrence and reform, it is deterrence that will be preferred. Giving an offender the punishment he deserves is thought to be the best way of deterrring him and the tarrif system takes these objectives in its stride, that is, the judges always have reform considerations in their mind when they are passing a sentence that will deter.

Where reform considerations are preferred the principle that punishment should fit the crime will clash with the objective of reform. The judges, therefore, combine the two objectives while awarding punishment. The overall attitude of the judges is reflected in the words of Lord Devlin.

> When the period has been fixed as justice demands, the law authorises and indeed encourages the penologist to use it for the work of reformation.... The sentence must not be longer than is justified by the gravity of the crime and must not fall below the least that justice demands.... The penologist's objective is to send the prisoner back into the world changed for the better. He may not always hope for complete reformation, but at least he does not want him to leave while there is still a reasonable chance that further treatment may improve his prospects. When these objectives clash, it is the just sentence which must prevail...."[114]

6.4 The Theory of Prevention

According to the prevention theory, the object of punishment is to incapacitate the offender from committing further crimes. "The protection of society from the offender's maraudings, even for a comparatively short time, is a frequent judicial justification of a sentence."[115] This too is one of the purposes of punishment listed on page 73.

In reality, the theory of prevention cannot be considered a separate theory, because it uses all the different approaches, including detterence, to prevent the commission of crime. This element

114. *The Judge,* 29–30 as quoted in Smith and Hogan, *Criminal Law,* 16.
115. Cross, *The English Sentencing System,* 135.

of prevention theory is in the minds of those who maintain that no single theory can yield perfect results. Punisment is a broad and general programme in which we should consider each important group of crime separately; yet, too much generalization often becomes ineffective.

6.5 General Conclusion: Integrative Approach

We would like to end this chapter with the words of Jerome Hall that appear to have more meaning than individual theories:

> If a theory of punishment took due account of the various problems indicated above, the outlook so far as scientific research is concerned, and consequently also with reference to the administration and reform of penal law, would be greatly altered. Attention could then be directed to carefully formulated, pertinent questions, *e.g.* within the limits set by the principle of legality, in what particular offenses, regarding which types of offender, in relation to what prevalent crime rates, available facilities and so on, should the peno-correctional treatment be determined and adjusted thus and so in order to preserve the maximum intrinsic and instrumental values?
>
> Despite the unusual difficulties which beset the problem of punishment, important progress has been made in recent years in the above direction. For example, it is now recognized that the "prevention of crime" and the "protection of society" are ends accepted by everyone, and that the reiteration of such slogans does not solve problems. It seems also to be widely agreed that involuntary incarceration is punishment regardless of the kindness of the administrators or the unexceptionable quality of the treatment program. And although there are unfortunate relapses, only infrequently does one find the punitive sanctions of civilized laws equated with vengeance or other merely emotional reactions or the cruel imposition of suffering as an end in itself. But the most important advance is that the inclusive theory of punishment has been gaining ground in recent years.[116]

116. Jerome Hall, *General Principles of Criminal Law,* 307–308.

Accordingly, what we need in Islamic law is an inclusive or integrative theory that requires different goals for each group of offences—*ḥudūd, qiṣāṣ* and *diyāt, ta'zīr*, and *siyāsah*—and within these for individual offences. Each punishment fixed or awarded must be adjusted in the light of an integrative programme.

REVIEW QUESTIONS

① Justify the theory of retribution in the light of arguments of Western writers as well as Muslim jurists.

② How does al-Sarakhsī justify the theory of deterrence—even for *qiṣāṣ*.

③ Formulate an integrative theory for law as well as Islamic law in the light of what Jerome Hall has said.

④ Is general deterrence against justice?

⑤ "To be punished for reform reasons is to be treated like a dog"—J. Mabbot. Comment in the light of the retributive theory of punishment.

⑥ The words of the Qur'ān are: "In *qiṣāṣ* there is life for you." Discuss in the light of the theories of punishment.

Part II

GENERAL PRINCIPLES OF CRIMINAL LAW

CHAPTER 7

ELEMENTS OF CRIME, CRIMINAL PROCESS AND BURDEN OF PROOF

The law condemns and punishes only actions within certain definite and narrow limits; it thereby justifies, in a way, all similar actions that lie outside those limits.

Leo Tolstoy,
What I Believe

7.1 Adversarial and Inquisitorial Processes

There are two procedural systems for delivering justice: the adversarial and the inquisitorial. We may also refer to them as the two models of justice systems. The distinctions drawn between the two systems focus on the functions performed by the judge and the extent of the role played by him in the legal proceedings. This distinction also examines the roles played by lawyers in the two systems. As an initial statement, we may say that "in a typical inquisitorial proceeding, the trial is dominated by a presiding judge, who determines the order in which evidence is taken and who evaluates the content of the gathered evidence .... without being constrained by strict rules in that respect."[117] As compared to this, in adversarial proceedings, "the case is organized and the facts are developed by the sole initiative of the parties. The process develops through the efforts of the litigants before a passive decision maker who reaches a decision on the sole basis of the evidence and

117. Francesco Parisil, "Rent-seeking Through Litigation: Adversarial and Inquisitorial Systems Compared," *International Review of Law and Economics* 22 (2002): 193.

motions presented by the litigants."[118] The inquisitorial system is followed in the civil law countries, while the adversarial system is followed in common law countries. Pakistan inherited the adversarial system from the United Kingdom. Islamic law, on the other hand, has had an inquisitorial system from the start. As more and more laws are Islamized, we might find ourselves moving towards a system that is inquisitorial in nature. It is also said that the adversarial system is more suited to an environment that is relatively stable and peaceful, while an inquisitorial serves an environment that has disturbances, or is at war, better. Without going into the merits of this view, it is suggested that it might be better to examine what system will be better for Pakistan. Further, it may be noted that in recent years, adversarial models have begun to incorporate some of the features of inquisitorial systems, especially in the area of Criminal Procedure; for example, the development of obligatory pre-trial case management processes. At the same time, inquisitorial models have also undergone significant reforms that incorporate elements of adversarial models. These developments highlight further the need for Pakistan to examine both models objectively and to determine its needs of the country in the light of Islamic law. In this section, we will merely list the main points of difference between the two sytems. The detailed study with reference to Pakistan will be undertaken in another text. The differences listed below in tabular form have been taken from the Law Commission of Teakamatuaoteture and the Ministry of Justice of New Zealand.

7.1.1 Responsibility for marshalling evidence for trial

In an **adversarial model,** responsibility for gathering evidence rests with the parties—police and defence—and an independent evaluation of that evidence by a neutral judge is left to the trial. In an **inquisitorial model,** criminal investigation, at least in serious cases, is typically overseen by either an "independent" prosecutor or an examining magistrate (in France termed a "juge d'instruction"). The prosecutor or examining magistrate can seek

118. Parisil, "Adversarial and Inquisitorial Systems Compared," 193.

particular evidence; direct lines of inquiry favourable to either prosecution or defence; interview complainants, witnesses and suspects; and ultimately determine whether there is sufficient evidence to take a case to trial.

7.1.2 Relative faith in the integrity of pre-trial processes

An **adversarial model** is based on mistrust in the reliability of the prosecution evidence. It proceeds on the assumption that mistaken verdicts of guilt can best be avoided by allowing the defence to test and counter that evidence at the trial itself, largely in the manner in which it chooses to do so. The trial is the exclusive forum for seeking out and determining the truth—or, perhaps more accurately, for determining whether there is a reasonable doubt as to guilt. An **inquisitorial model** has faith in the integrity of pre-trial processes (overseen by the prosecutor or examining magistrate) to distinguish between reliable and unreliable evidence; to detect flaws in the prosecution case; and to identify evidence that is favourable to the defence. In many jurisdictions, this culminates in the preparation of a "dossier" for the trial court that outlines all aspects of the case and forms the basis for the trial itself. Pre-trial processes are therefore an indispensable part of the process for seeking out the truth. By the time a case reaches trial, there is a greater presumption of guilt than in an adversary model.

7.1.3 The extent of discretion

Because in an **adversarial model** decision making is left largely in the hands of the parties, there is a recognised prosecutorial discretion not to proceed with the case, even when there is evidence to support a criminal charge. There is also an ability, recognised in statute, for the defendant to plead guilty and avoid a trial.

In an **inquisitorial model,** discretion is much more limited. In some jurisdictions, "the legality principle" dictates, in theory if not in practice, that prosecution must take place in all cases in which sufficient evidence exists of the guilt of the subject. Moreover, there was traditionally no such thing in civil law jurisdictions as a plea of guilty. Regardless of the accused's wishes, trial processes continued, albeit on a sometimes more accelerated path.

7.1.4 The nature of the trial process

In an **adversarial model** all parties determine the witnesses they call and the nature of the evidence they give, and the opposing party has the right to cross-examine. The court's role is confined to overseeing the process by which evidence is given (to ensure that it is within the rules) and then weighing up that evidence to determine whether there is a reasonable doubt. There are strict rules to prevent the admission of evidence that may prejudice or mislead the fact finder. In an **inquisitorial model,** the conduct of the trial is largely in the hands of the court. With the dossier of evidence as its starting point, the trial judge determines what witnesses to call and the order in which they are to be heard, and assumes the dominant role in questioning them. Cross examination as we know it does not exist, although the parties and their counsel are generally permitted to ask questions. There are far fewer rules of evidence and much more information available to the court at the outset. The offender s criminal history, for example, may be read to the court before the trial begins.

7.1.5 The role of the victim

In an **adversarial model,** the victim is largely relegated to the role of witness. They have no recognised status in either the pre-trial investigation or the trial itself. In an **inquisitorial model,** on the other hand, victims have a more recognised role. In some jurisdictions they have a formal role in the pre-trial investigative stage, including a recognised right to request particular lines of inquiry or to participate in interviews by the examining magistrate. At the trial itself, they generally have independent standing. Although this is partly for the purposes of claiming compensation, they are sometimes also permitted to ask questions of witnesses.

7.2 Criminal Process

Criminal procedure in Pakistan is governed by the Criminal Procedure Code, 1898, except where another law has provided a special procedure as in some of the the Hudood laws. The other two laws that come into play in an essential manner are the Pakistan Penal Code, 1860 and the Qanun-e-Shahadat Order, 1984. The PPC is the main law that defines crimes and deals with the substantive part of the bulk of the criminal law.

The Cr.P.C. is a comprehensive and exhaustive procedural law for conducting a criminal trials in Pakistan and it covers, among other things, the manner for collection of evidence, examination of witnesses, interrogation of accused, arrests, safeguards and procedures to be adopted by the Police and the Courts, bail, process of criminal trial, method of conviction, and the rights of the accused for a fair trial.

The source for the authority of all the above laws is the Constitution of Pakistan, 1973. In addition to this, the Constitution contains a number of controlling provisions of the criminal law and procedure. It provides, for example, Article 10 speaks about safeguards as to arrest and detention, [119] while Article 10A talks about the right to fair trial and about due process.[120] Likewise Article 12 protects against retrospective punishment,[121] while Article 13

119. (1) No person who is arrested shall be detained in custody without being informed, as soon as may be, of the grounds for such arrest, nor shall he be denied the right to consult and be defended by a legal practitioner of his choice.
(2) Every person who is arrested and detained in custody shall be produced before a magistrate within a period of twenty-four hours of such arrest, excluding the time necessary for the journey from the place of arrest to the court of the nearest magistrate, and no such person shall be detained in custody beyond the said period without the authority of a magistrate.

120. For the determination of his civil rights and obligations or in any criminal charge against him a person shall be entitled to a fair trial and due process.

121. (1) No law shall authorize the punishment of a person—
(a) for an act or omission that was not punishable by law at the time

prohibits double jeopardy, as does section 403 of the CrPC. It has, therefore, rightly been said that by guaranteeing some of the important human fundamental rights, the Constitutional provides a veritable mini-code of criminal procedure and fair practices in the criminal law.

As stated for civil procedure, Pakistan following UK follows the adversarial system. Thus, in general, the onus of proof is on the State (that is, the Prosecution) to prove the case against the accused. Further, the allegations against the accused must be proved beyond reasonable doubt, for otherwise the accused will be presumed to be innocent. Today, the onus of proof may have been placed on the accused person in cases of terrorism in the interest of national security. It may be added here in praise of our judiciary that the courts are every watchful of the rights of the accused in criminal cases. In doing so, they may seek help from other Articles of the Constitution, especially the fundamental rights.

Criminal procedure is complex business and we can merely indicate a few steps that are involved. A few terms used by this law may be helpful. Thus, the major stages in criminal pro procedure are the following:

- Investigation and Inquiry
- Prosecution
- Trial

The participants involved in these three stages are: Police; Prosecutor; Defence Counsel; and the Courts.

7.2.1 Investigation

According to section 4(l), the term "Investigation" includes all the proceedings under this Code for the collection of evidence con-

---

of the act or omission; or
(b) for an offence by a penalty greater than, or of a kind different from, the penalty prescribed by law for that offence at the time the offence was committed.

ducted by a police officer or by any person (other than a Magistrate) who is authorised by a Magistrate in this behalf. Here a distinction may be drawn between "cognizable" and "non-cognizable" offences. A cognizable offence or case is defined as "an offence in which a police officer can arrest without a warrant," while a "non-cognizable Offence" is "an offence in which a police officer has no authority to arrest without a warrant." (Section 4(f) and (n)). A related classification into bailable and non bailable offences. A bailable offence is one in which bail can be claimed as a matter of right and can be given by the police. Thus, if a person is arrested in a non-cognizable case, the police my grant bail. In a non-bailable offence that is cognizable, bail cannot be granted as a matter of right, except on the orders of a competent court. This is just a rough idea, and whether an offence is bailable or non-bailable, and cognizable or non-cognizable is spelled out in detail in the 1st Schedule of Cr.P.C.

The F.I.R or the First Information Report is a report made to the police in case of commission of a cognizable offences and is in reality the first step in the process of the investigation of a cognizable offence by police. The investigation process is started in one of the following ways: (1) On complaint, report, or knowledge of the commission of a cognizable offence, a police officer can investigate such cognizable offence even without the orders of a Magistrate. (2) In case of inaction of a police officer to investigate a cognizable offence, a criminal complaint can be filed before a Magistrate for taking cognizance of such offence, and on such complaint, the Magistrate himself can take cognizance of the case and undertake the inquiry, or in the alternative order the police to register an F.I.R and investigate the offence. (3) In the case of non-cognizable offences, the police are not obliged to investigate, and the judicial process can be started by filing a criminal complaint before the competent court.

Here it may be noted that a person may apply for bail before arrest or anticipatory bail. It means that a person, who apprehends arrest on a wrong accusation of committing a non-bailable offence, can apply before a competent court for a direction to police to immediately release such a person on bail in the event of arrest.

7.2.2 Prosecution

The role of the prosecution covers the entire criminal process and cannot be elaborated here. Due to its significance recent legislation in the Provinces has established an independent criminal prosecuting service. Prosecution envelops the entire art of the criminal lawyer, and more. The role of defence counsel is equally, if not more, important. Both lawyers are considered the officers of court.

7.2.3 Trial

The trial is undertaken through the adversarial process. As it is public law one of the parties is the state, while the accused is the other party. Due to the Islamization of laws, private parties too have some role in certain cases along with the state. The classes of courts, described in the CrPC, become important to see where the trial will be held. The powers of courts laid down in the Code also assume great significance. As state, it is a constitutional requirement that the trial be fair and that due process be observed. The meaning of fairness acquires importance, and the courts keep on dilating upon its exact impact and scope.

The student will later learn the difference between summary and regular trials, as he will understand the pre-trial steps including the determination of the place of trial. The meaning of cognizance of offence also assumes great significance. The attendance of the accused and the supplying of copies of various statements recorded is extremely important. Trial is to commence in open court and it is the duty of the judge to prevment abuse of delay through adjournments and other methods.

The charge is framed and the process of recording evidence, the examination of witnesses, and arguments are undertaken meticulously. The mode of taking and recording evidence is given in Chapter XXV Cr.P.C. After the recording of evidence, the examination of witnesses and the accused, and arguments, the final order/judgement is made. This is the conclusion of the trial and may lead to the conviction or acquittal. Conviction is followed by sentence. There are detailed procedures for appeals and other processes after final judgement, which the student will come across during his study.

7.3 Criminal Liability and Elements of a Crime

Criminal liability is based on the principle that a man is not criminally liable for his conduct unless the prescribed state of mind is also present. This principle is frequently stated in the form of a Latin maxim: *Actus non facit reum nisi mens sit rea.* Properly translated, this means "An act does not make a man guilty of a crime, unless his mind be also guilty."[122] The principle is not understood in the same meaning as it was used in medieval times; it has been defined and redefined. A famous writer says: "The full implications of the requirements of *mens rea* cannot be appreciated until not only the chapter and the entire book but many others have been studied."[123]

Culpability under Western legal systems, today, is founded upon certain basic premises that are more or less strictly observed by legislatures when formulating the substantive law of crimes. The courts keep these basic premises in view during trial. The same rules are followed in Pakistan. Consequently, **the prosecution is generally required to prove the following elements of a criminal offence:**

1. **Actus Reus (guilty act):** A physical act (or unlawful omission) by the defendant; in reality, a collection of elements other than the mental element, collectively referred to as the *actus reus.* (See the discussion of *actus reus* below at page 115).

2. **Mens Rea (guilty mind):** The state of mind or intent of the defendant at the time of his act;

122. Smith and Hogan, *Criminal Law,* 32 fn. 6.
123. Cross and Jones, *Introduction to Criminal Law,* 20.

3. **Concurrence:** The physical act and the mental state existing at the same time.

It is important to note that the burden of proving these elements beyond reasonable doubt rests upon the prosecution. The position in Islamic law is similar. There may be cases where *mens rea* (*'amd* or *qaṣd jinā'ī*) is not relevant. These are usually cases of strict liability and will be discussed under that topic. (See page 141).

7.4 The Nature of the Elements

The attempt to extract elements common to all crimes has its limitations and problems. The reader should realize that the elements are most helpful when they are used to study specific crimes, but are likely to lead the discussion into details of exceptions and provisos when studied in an abstract all embracing sense. The following points should be kept in mind while studying the elements of crime:

1. **The analysis into *actus reus* and *mens rea* is for convenience of exposition only.**[124] The only concept known to the law is the crime and the crime exists when the *actus reus* and *mens rea* coincide.[125] Once it is decided that an element is an ingredient of an offence, there is no legal significance in the classification of it as part of the *actus reus* or the *mens rea*.[126] It is, perhaps, for this reason that Muslim jurists did not discuss the elements in an abstract form. They did, however, discuss the elements within specific crimes. Modern writers use terms like *rukn mādī* and *qaṣd jinā'ī* to describe the elements. There is nothing Islamic about these terms; they have been borrowed from the Egyptian law. The word usually used by Muslim jurists for criminal intention is *'amd*, which is found in the Qur'ān.

124. Smith and Hogan, *Criminal Law,* 30.
125. Ibid.
126. Ibid.

2. **In law, the bringing about of the *actus reus* implies no judgment as to its moral or legal quality.** In Islamic law, on the other hand, there is a definite judgment as to the moral quality of an offence involving criminal intention and is tied in with expiation (*kaffārah*).
3. **It is not always possible to separate the *actus reus* from *mens rea*.** Sometimes a word which describes the *actus reus* implies a mental element. There are many offences of "possession" of proscribed objects and it has always been recognized that possession consists in a mental as well as a physical element. The same is true of words like "permits," "appropriates," "cultivates" and many more.[127] The significance of this is that any mental element which is part of the *actus reus* is necessarily a part of the offence.
4. **It is extremely difficult to draw out the elements that are common to all offences.** This has already been explained above.

7.5 Burden of Proof

The general rule for the criminal law the general rule is that the prosecution has the burden of proof, and the burden is to prove guilt "beyond a reasonable doubt." This springs from another rule: Everyone charged with a criminal offence shall be presumed innocent until proven guilty. This is related to the due process Article of the Constitution. Thus, in 1970 the U.S. Supreme Court declared that the Constitution required the reasonable doubt rule in criminal cases. In the case of *In re Winship,* 397 U.S. 358 (1970), the Court held that the "Due Process Clause protects the accused against conviction except upon proof beyond a reasonable doubt of every fact necessary to constitute the crime with which he is charged." We have mentioned this here as the prosecution is required primarily to prove the elements of the case discussed below. The details will be studied in individual crimes and in criminal procedure.

127. Ibid.

It may be mentioned here that the rule may apply to certain types of juvenile delinquency proceedings, even though they may not be classified as criminal. Further, it may be that despite the strict requirement of the prosecution proving guilt beyond a reasonable doubt, courts may require defendants to prove such issues as self-defence, duress, insanity, entrapment, and mistake.

CHAPTER 8

ACTUS REUS AND CAUSATION

The law embodies the story of a nation's development through many centuries, and it cannot be dealt with as if it contained only the axioms and corollaries of a book of mathematics.

Oliver Wendell Holmes, Jr.,
The Common Law

8.1 Physical Act: *Actus Reus*

8.1.1 The meaning of *actus reus*

Each crime must have an *actus reus,* ie, the act defined and prohibited by law and declared an offence. For this purpose, an act is defined as a bodily movement. A thought is not an act. Therefore, bad thoughts alone cannot constitute a crime. Note, however, that speech, unlike thought, is an act that can cause liability, eg, perjury. The *actus reus* includes **all the elements in the definition of the crime, except the accused's mental element.** It follows, therefore, that the *actus reus* is not merely an act. Further, it may consist in a "state of affairs," not including an act at all. Perhaps, it is for this reason that §40 PPC defines offence as a "thing." The *actus reus* itself may be said to consist of the following elements:

1. **Conduct:** Conscious voluntary bodily movement. The *actus reus* requires proof of an act. An act may include, in some cases, an omission (conduct) or failure to act when the law imposes such a duty. §32 PPC says that "[i]n every part of this Code, except2 when a contrary intention appears from the context, words which refer to acts done extend also to

illegal omissions." §33 says: "The word 'act' denotes as well a series of acts as a single act: the word 'omission' denotes as well a series of omissions as a single omission."

2. **The consequences of the act:** The *actus reus* must lead to the prohibited result. For example, if D hurls a stone, being reckless whether he injures anyone, he is guilty of a crime if the stone strikes P but of no offence if by chance no one is injured. Nevertheless, some acts may not have a result, and the act itself constitutes the crime, as in perjury. It is an offence as soon as the statement is made. It is to be noted that it is the conduct and not the result that is the *actus reus.* A dead man with a knife in his back is not the *actus reus* of murder. It is putting the knife in the back thereby causing the death which is the *actus reus.*

3. **Circumstances in which the act takes place:** The circumstaces may constitute a "state of affairs" that make the act of the accused unlawful. For example, some situations contemplated under §144 PPC. The presence of the accused is an act, while the existence of the unlawful assembly is the state of affairs. Sometimes a particular state of mind on the part of the victim may be required. If D is prosecuted for the offence of *zinā bi'l-jabr* or rape not liable to *ḥadd,* it must be shown that P did not consent to the act of sexual intercourse.

"The *actus reus* is made up, generally, but not invariably, of conduct and sometimes its consequences and also of the circumstances in which the conduct takes place (or which constitute the state of affairs) in so far as they are relevant."[128] It is to be noted that circumstances as well as consequences are relevant if they are included in the definition of the crime.[129] It also shows that it is only by looking at the definition of the crime that we can see what circumstances are material to the *actus reus.* What is usually not mentioned in the definition are circumstances which, if they exist,

128. Ibid., 31–32.
129. Ibid., 32

amount in law to a justification or excuse, and in such a case no crime is committed. There is no *actus reus*. In such cases, the doctrines have to be added to the definition, as emphasised earlier. (See page 28).

8.1.2 Rules for the *actus reus*

8.1.2.1 The *actus reus* must be proved

It must be shown by the prosecution that an *actus reus* does in fact exist. It is important to note that *mens rea* may exist without an *actus reus*, but if there is no *actus reus* there can be no crime.

> (1) D may believe that the property he is appropriating belongs to P, but he cannot be guilty of theft unless the property *belongs to someone*. It may be noted, however, that the definition of theft liable to *ḥadd* does not include ownership as a condition, although the earlier jurists unanimously maintain that ownership by someone is a necessary ingredient of the offence. The provision avoids the difficulty of ownership by a juristic persons, a concept that traditional Islamic law does not recognize.
>
> (2) §494 of the PPC prohibits marriage during the lifetime of the existing spouse when the new marriage is void because of the existing marriage. If D intends to marry during the lifetime of P, but unknown to him she is dead. There is no *actus reus* here.
>
> (3) D may assault P with the intent to ravish her but, if in fact she consents, his act cannot amount to rape. The *actus reus* of rape does not exist, but that of *zinā* does.

There are two interesting British cases that highlight the rule that an *actus reus* must be established.

R v Deller (1952) 36 Cr. App. R. 184. C.C.A.

> The defendant induced a man to buy his car representing (*inter alia*) that it was free from encumberances. The defendant had in fact executed a document which purported to mortgage the car to a finance company and must have thought that he was telling a lie. He was charged under the Larceny Act with obtaining by false pretences. It became apparent that the document was void for lack of registration

> and thus the car was free from encumberances. The conviction was quashed by the Court of Criminal Appeal on the basis that although the defendant had the *mens rea,* there was no *actus reus.* Although he thought he had achieved all the consequences involved in the *actus reus* of the complete crime, the consequences turned out not to be a crime because the pretences were not false (Hilbery J.)
>
> *R v Dadson* (1850) 2 Den. 35, C.C.R.
>
> The defendant, a police constable, was employed to keep watch on a copse and on seeing a man carry stolen wood from the copse called on him to stop. The man ran away and the defendant fired at him and wounded him in the leg. The man had been convicted summarily of stealing wood on numerous occasions and such stealing after two convictions was a "felony." It was assumed to be lawful to wound an escaping felon in order to arrest him. However, the defendant had no knowledge of the previous convictions and therefore was unaware that the man was a "felon." Erle J. directed the jury that the alleged felony, being unknown to the prisoner, constituted no justification. On appeal it was held that the defendent was rightly convicted, because he did not know that the man was committing a felony at the time (Pollok C.B.)

Glanville Williams maintained that the two cases are inconsistent as decided. In the Deller case, the court reached its decision on the basis of the facts as they actually were—not on the facts as D believed them to be at the time he committed the alleged crime. In the Dadson case, on the other hand, the court acted on the basis of what was supposed to be D's reasonable belief and not on the facts as they actually were. He said that there was no *actus reus* in either case.

Smith and Hogan disagree with this line of argument and maintain that this will lead to a very narrow doctrine. It is important to distinguish, they say, between the types of defence that may be raised. In the first case, D merely denies the existence of an element (other than *mens rea*) in the definition of the crime. If D makes out the defence he certainly cannot be convicted whatever his state of mind. In the second case, D admits that all the elements in the definition of the crime have been established and goes on to assert other facts which afford him a defence in law. This would mean that the prosecution have to prove the *mens rea* as well as the non-existence of external exonerating facts.

Would you agree with Glanville Williams or with Smith and Hogan? As the second case would invoke *qiṣāṣ,* do you think the prosecution has to prove the non-existence of *shubhah fi'l-fi'l,* an external fact?

8.1.2.2 The Act Must Be Voluntary

The defendant's act must be voluntary in the sense that it must be a conscious exercise of the will. The rationale for this rule is that an involuntary act will not be deterred by punishment. The following acts are not considered "voluntary" and therefore cannot be the basis for criminal liability:

1. Conduct that is not the product of the actor's determination. A shoves B into C, with the result that C falls to his death. Can B be held criminally liable for C's death? No. According to Muslim jurists, B is an instrument (weapon of aggression) in the hands of A, but what would be A's libility in this case?
2. Reflexive or convulsive acts.
3. Acts performed while the defendant was either unconscious or asleep unless the defendant knew that he might fall asleep or become unconscious and engage in dangerous behaviour.

What would be the liability of the defendant in the last two cases under Islamic law? Will the defendant be liable for *diyah* if the acts result in someone's death or injury? What offence would be committed, if any?

The main question that is faced is whether voluntariness of D's conduct should be regarded as part of the *actus reus* or part of the *mens rea.* The effect of this distinction is that if it is part of the *mens rea,* an involuntary act will be no defence in cases of strict liability. On the other hand, if voluntariness is part of the *actus reus,* it will have to be proved even in these cases. Some writers feel that this distinction is not important as even in crimes of strict liability a limited degree of *mens rea* must be proved, and the jurist may if he chooses classify voluntariness of the accused's act as part of the limited degree of *mens rea*.[130]

Automatism: Most of the cases falling under the voluntary act concern automatism. A person is an automaton when he has no control over his muscular movements. Automatism is divided into different types by writers: automatism due to insanity; automatism due to other reasons; and self-induced automatism. When automatism results from self-induced intoxication or by the defendant's fault it will apparently be no defence. The plea of insanity, on the other hand, is avoided by defendants as it usually results in going to a mental institution at the pleasure of authorities. However, where the alleged automatism arises from a "disease of the mind," the defence is one of insanity and the onus of proof is on the accused. Where it arises from some cause other than disease of the mind, the onus of proof is on the prosecution. What is a disease of mind is a question of law. The following British cases explain the point to some extent:

1. In *Kemp* where D alleged that he acted involuntarily because he suffered from arteriosclerosis which cut off the supply of blood to his brain, Devlin J held that he had set up the defence of insanity.
2. In *Charlson,* Barry J treated an allegation of automatism arising from a cerebral tumor as a defence to be disproved beyond reasonable doubt by the prosecution. This case is irreconcilable with the previous one.
3. Acts done while sleeping, sleepwalking, in a hypoglycaemic episode or under concussion have been regarded as non-insane automatism.
4. External factors such as violence, drugs, including anaesthetics, alcohol and hypnotic influences cannot be said to be due to disease.

Automatism has narrow limits as a defence. It is to be confined to acts done while unconscious and to spasms, reflex actions and convulsions. The common law never recognized "irresistable impulse" as a defence even when it arose from insanity (in England,

130. Smith and Hogan, *Criminal Law,* 37.

an irresistable craving for drink is not a defence to a charge of stealing alcohol).

Involuntariness not arising from automatism. It may happen that a person may have full control over his body and muscular movements, yet he may have no control over the events he is passing through.

> A driver's brakes fail without his fault and he runs over a pedestrian on a crossing. Although it is said that this offence is absolute requiring no offence of negligence, it was held in *Burns v Bidder* (1967) 2 QB 227 that such a driver has a defence. The court equated the driver's situation with that of one stunned by a swarm of bees, disabled by epilepsy, or propelled by vehicle hitting his car from behind.

This shows that voluntariness is essential even in so-called crimes of absolute liability. The general rule should be that the defendant is not criminally liable for events over which he has no control.

8.1.2.3 Causation: The act should be causative

If the definition of an *actus reus* requires the occurrence of certain consequences it is necessary to prove that it was the conduct of the accused that caused those consequences to occur. When the defendant is charged with any "result" crime, the prosecution must prove that his acts or omissions caused the prohibited consequence. For example, in murder or manslaughter, it is necessary to prove that the defendant, by his acts or omissions, caused the victim's death. If the victim dies because of some other cause, then the offence has not been committed even though all the other elements of the offence, including the *mens rea,* are present. The defendant, however, may be liable for attempt.[131]

In *qatl-i-'amd* or *qatl-i-khaṭa',* it is necessary to prove that the act caused the death. If the death came about solely through some other cause then the crime is not committed. Causation is called *sababīyah* in Arabic. See the illustrations under the relevant sections of the PPC.

131. White (1910) 2 KB 124.

8.1.3 A "State of Affairs" as an *actus reus*

The definition of a crime may be formulated in such a way that it can be committed although there is no "act." There is no need for a "willed muscular movement," and it may be enough if a specified "state of affairs" is proved to exist. These offences are sometimes called "status" or "situation" offences. §§400 & 401 of the PPC belonging to a gang of dacoits or a gang of thieves may be treated as examples of status offences.

8.1.4 Omission as an "Act"

Although most crimes are committed by affirmative action rather than by nonaction, a defendant's failure to act will result in criminal liability provided three requirements are satisfied.

1. **There is a legal duty to act.** The defendant must have a legal duty to act under the circumstances. A legal duty to act can arise from the following sources.

   a) A statute, such as that of filing an income tax return or of reporting an accident.

   b) A contract obligating the defendant to act, such as that entered into by a lifeguard or a nurse.

   c) The relationship between the defendant and the victim, which may be sufficiently close to create a duty.

      - A parent has the duty to prevent physical harm to his or her children.
      - A spouse has the duty to prevent harm to his or her spouse.

   d) The voluntary assumption of care by the defendant of the victim. Although in general there is no common law duty to help someone in distress, once aid is rendered, the good Samaritan may be held criminally liable for not satisfying a reasonable standard of care.

   e) The creation of peril by the defendant.

      - Believing the B can swim, A pushes B into a pool. It becomes apparent that B cannot swim, but A takes no steps to help B. B drowns. Was A's failure to attempt a rescue an "act" upon which liability can be based? Yes.

2. **There is a knowledge of facts giving rise to duty.** As a general rule, the duty to act arises when the defendant is aware of the facts creating the duty to act (e.g., the parent must know that his child is drowning before his failure to rescue the child will make him liable). However, in some situations the law will impose a duty to learn the facts (e.g., a lifeguard asleep at his post would still have a legal duty to aid a drowning swimmer).

3. **It is reasonably possible to perform the duty.** It must be reasonably possible for the defendant to perform the duty or to obtain the help of others in performing it. A parent who is unable to swim is under no duty to jump in the water to attempt to save his drowning child.

8.1.5 Possession as an "Act"

Criminal statutes that penalize the possession of contraband generally require only that the defendant have control of the item for a long enough period to have had an opportunity to terminate the possession. The defendant must be aware of his possession of the object but need not be aware of its illegality.

Review Questions

① What is performance of contract? Discuss the law as to who may perform a contract, and under what conditions a contract need not be performed. (2005) time and place of performance (2005 supp.) when there are joint promisors (2007 supp.).

② What do you understand by reciprocal promises? Discuss the rules governing the performance of such promises. (2008 supp.).

③ How and in what order should reciprocal promises be performed? (2003).

④ State briefly the law governing the appropriation of payments. (2002) (2004).

CHAPTER 9

MENS REA

There is no such thing as justice—in or out of court.

Clarence Darrow, 1936

9.1 Mental State (*Mens Rea*)

Oliver Wendell Holmes, in his famous book *Common Law,* has traced the growth of fault liability in the West. The Old Testament, for example, maintained that "[i]f an ox gore a man, the owner of the ox shall be quit, but the ox will surely be stoned." Fault was attributed to the ox. Likewise, stones and swords of steel were cast beyond the borders when liability was assigned to them. This was followed by a very long period of strict liability that did not take into account a blameworthy state of the mind. Beginning in the 12th century, it took more than four hundred years for England to switch over to a legal system that took intention into consideration.

As compared to this, the Qur'ān itself recognized intention (*'amd*), negligence and strict liability for the fixation of criminal liability.

9.1.1 The meaning of *mens rea*

Mens rea is a technical term, and its translation as a "guilty mind" is considered misleading.[132] Technically, the possible mental attitudes a man may have with respect to the *actus reus* of a crime are: intention; recklessness; negligence; and blameless inadvertence. We shall examine these terms briefly.

132. Ibid., 47.

Mental States
- Intention
- Recklessness
- Negligence
- Blameless Inadvertence

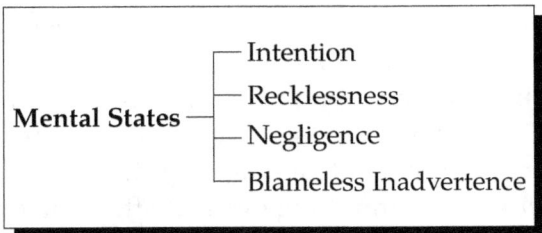

9.1.1.1 Intention

Where the definition of the *actus reus* of the offence charged requires the accused's conduct to produce a particular consequence he has a sufficient mental state as to that consequence if he intended it to occur.

1. **Direct and oblique intention.** There are two types of intention with regard to prohibited consequences, "direct" intention and "oblique" intention. The distinction was drawn by Jeremy Bentham.[133] Direct intention has been defined by the courts as "a decision to bring about, insofar as it lies within the accused's power, a particular consequence, no matter whether the accused desired that consequence of his act or not." As compared to this, a consequence of a person's conduct is said to have been obliquely intended by him when, although he had not intended to bring it about, insofar as it lay within his power, it was **forseen** by him as a certain or probable side effect of something.

   Again foresight is divided into two types: *foresight of certainty* and *foresight of probability*.

   > If F, who wishes to collect isurance on an air cargo, puts a time bomb on the aircraft to blow it up in flight, realizing that it is certain that those on board will be killed by the explosion, he acts with an oblique intention in a legal sense with a foresight of certainty.

133. Cross and Jones, *Introduction to Criminal Law*, 29.

2. **Further or ulterior intent.** A crime is frequently so defined that the *mens rea* includes an intention to produce some further consequence beyond the *actus reus* of the crime in question. §382 of the PPC which provides punishment for "theft after preparation made for causing death, hurt or restraint in order to the committing of the theft," is an example. The actual commission of the other acts (death, hurt etc.) is no part of the *actus reus*. Where such an ulterior intent is to be proved, it is sometimes referred to as "specific intent." Cross and Jones have pointed out that this term should be regarded with caution. In the United States, however, it appears to be used frequently by courts, where it may be used in slightly different sense. This is discussed below.

Specific intent and general intent: United States. As pointed out the terms specific intent and general intent, it appears, are used in a slightly different sense as compared to the meaning given to these terms in England. The use is summarized below.

1. **Specific Intent Crime.** If the definition of a crime requires not only the doing of an act, but the doing of it with a specific intent or objective, the crime is a "specific intent" crime. It is necessary to identify specific intent for two reasons:
    a) **Need for Proof.** The existence of a specific intent cannot be inferred from the doing of the act. The prosecution must produce evidence tending to prove the existence of the specific intent.
    b) **Applicability of Certain Defences.** Some defences, such as voluntary intoxication and unreasonable mistake of fact, apply only to specific intent crimes.
2. **Enumeration of Specific Intent Crimes.** The major specific intent crimes and the intent they require in the United States are as follows:
    a) *Solicitation (instigation):* The intent to have the person solicited commit the crime;
    b) *Attempt:* The intent to complete the crime;
    c) *Conspiracy:* The intent to have the crime completed;

d) *Premeditation:* First degree premeditated murder (where so defined by statute);
e) *Assault:* Intent to commit a battery;
f) *Larceny and robbery:* The intent to permanently deprive the other of his interest in the property taken;
g) *Burglary:* Intent to commit a felony in the dwelling;
h) *Forgery:* Intent to defraud;
i) *False pretences:* Intent to defraud; and
j) *Embezzlement:* Intent to defraud.

3. **General intent:** Generally, all crimes require "general intent," which is an awareness of all factors constituting the crime; i.e., defendant must be aware that he is acting in the proscribed way and that any attendant circumstances required by the crime are likely to be present. Thus, to commit the crime of false imprisonment, D must be aware that he is confining a person, and that the confinement has not been specifically authorized by law or validly consented to by the person confined.

Transferred Intent or Transferred Malice. If a defendant intended a harmful result to a particular person or object and, in trying to carry out that intent, caused a similar harmful result to another person or object, his intent will be transferred from the intended person or object to the one actually harmed. Any defences or mitigating circumstances that the defendant could have asserted against the intended victim (e.g., self-defence, provocation) will also be transferred in most cases. The doctrine of transferred intent most commonly applies to homicide, battery, and arson. It does not apply to attempt.

A shoots at B, intending to kill him. Because of bad aim, he hits C, killing him. Is A guilty of C's murder? Yes. His intent to kill B will be transferred to C. Note that A may also be guilty of the attempted murder of B.

A shoots at B, intending to kill him. He hits C, only wounding him. While A may be guilty of attempted murder of B, is he also guilty of attempted murder of C? No. Transferred intent does not apply to attempt.

In Islamic law, the Ḥanbalī school acknowledges transferred malice, but the majority of the schools are reluctant to do so.

Motive and Intention Distinguished—Motive does not affect liability. The motive for a crime is distinct from the intent to commit it. A motive is the reason or explanation underlying the offence. It is generally held that motive is immaterial to substantive criminal law. A good motive will not excuse a criminal act. On the other hand, a lawful act done with bad motive will not be punished.

> An impoverished woman steals so that her hungry children may eat. Despite her noble motive—feeding her children—the woman could be held criminally liable for her acts because her intent was to steal. (Note: *Ḥadd* cannot be applied in this case.)

Sometimes, when we speak of motive, we mean an emotion such as jealousy or greed, and sometimes we mean a species of intention.

> D intends (a) to put poison in his uncle's tea, (b) to cause his uncle's death and (c) to inherit his money. We would normally say that (c) is his motive, which is also intended if we look at the "desired consequences" test. The reason why it is considered merely a motive is that it is a consequence ulterior to the *mens rea* and *actus reus*.[134]

Where motive is relevant. In some exceptional cases motive is relevant.

1. **In a prosecution for libel,** if the civil law defences of fair comment or qualified privilege are available at all, they may be defeated by proof of motive in the sense of spite or ill-will.[135]

2. **As evidence,** motive is always relevant. Thus, if the prosecution can prove that D had a motive for committing the crime, they may do so since the existence of a motive makes it more likely that D in fact did commit it. Men do not always act without a motive.[136]

134. Smith and Hogan, *Criminal Law,* 67.
135. Ibid.
136. Ibid., 67–68.

3. **Motive is important again when the question of punishment is in issue.** When the law allows the judge a discretion in sentencing, he will obviously be more leniently disposed towards the convicted person who acted with a good motive. In other cases, it may help in the commutation of a sentence.[137]

9.1.1.2 Recklessness

In many offences recklessness, either as to the consequences required for the *actus reus* or as to the requisite circumstances of it or as to some other risk, suffices for criminal liability as opposed to some other mental state such as intention.[138] Since 1981 (after the decision in *Caldwell*), in England recklessness is understood in two different legal senses: subjective recklessness and *Caldwell* recklessness. Both are concerned with the taking of unjustified risk.

Subjective recklessness is the conscious taking of an unjustified risk. In such a case, the defendant forsees that the consequence in question may result and it is unreasonable for him to take the risk of it occurring. The *Caldwell* recklessness occurs when a person is reckless even when he has not given any thought to the possibility of there being any such risk.[139]

> In *Cunningham*, D tore a gas meter from the wall of the cellar of an unoccupied house to steal the money in it. He left the gas gushing out. It seeped into a neighbouring house and was inhaled by P whose life was endangered. D was convicted, but the on appeal the conviction was quashed. The reasoning was that in such cases "it is not sufficient that, if D had stopped to think, it would have been obvious to him that there was a risk. He must actually know of the existence of the risk and deliberately take it."
>
> In *Caldwell*, it was decided that when the statute uses the word "reckless" a different test applies. A person is reckless "if (1) he does an act which in fact creates an obvious risk

137. Ibid., 68.
138. Cross and Jones, *Introduction to Criminal Law*, 37.
139. Ibid., 40.

> that property would be destroyed or damaged *and* (2) when he does the act he either has not given any thought to the possibility of there being any such risk or has or has recognized that there was some risk involved and has nonetheless gone on to do it."[140]

9.1.1.3 Negligence

"Before *Caldwell* it was possible, in England, to draw a clear distinction between recklessness and negligence. Recklessness was the *conscious* taking of unjustified risk, negligence the *inadvertent* taking of an unjustified risk. If D was aware of the risk and decided to take it, he was reckless; if he was unaware of the risk, but ought to have been aware of it, he was negligent."[141]

This statement, however, does not apply to all cases. For example, D may wrongly conclude that there is no risk in his act, or that it is so small a risk that it would have been justifiable to take it. "This is now the hallmark of a crime of negligence."[142]

9.1.2 Basic *mens rea*

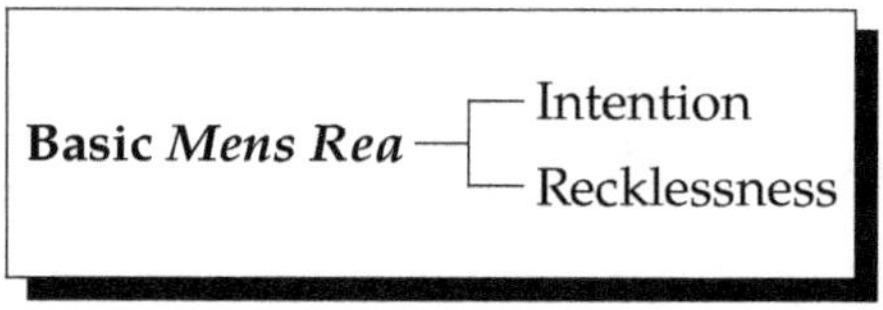

From the range of mental attitudes discussed above, it is obvious that the most blameworthy state of mind, with respect to an *actus reus,* is intention. This is followed by recklessness, negligence and blameless inadvertence, in that order.[143] To determine guilt, a line needs to be drawn somewhere within this range. The common law, though not always, drew the line between recklessness and negligence. The reckless man was liable, the negligent man was not. Basic *mens rea* would include intention and recklessness

140. Smith and Hogan, *Criminal Law,* 53–54.
141. Ibid., 57.
142. Ibid.
143. Ibid., 58.

with respect to all those circumstances and consequences of the accused's act (or state of affairs) which constitute the *actus reus* of the crime in question.[144]

9.2 Concurrence of *Mens Rea* With the *Actus Reus*

The defendant must have had the intent necessary for the crime at the time he committed the act constituting the crime. In addition, the intent must have actuated the act.

> A decides to kill B. While driving to the store to purchase a gun for this purpose, A negligently runs over B and kills him. Is A guilty of murder? No, because although at the time A caused B's death he had the intent to do so, this intent did not prompt the act resulting in B's death (i.e., A's poor driving).

The following rules are important:[145]

1. The *mens rea* must coincide in point of time with the act which causes the *actus reus*. The above example illustrates this.
2. Where the *actus reus* is a continuing act, it is sufficient that the defendant has *mens rea* during its continuance though not at the moment the *actus reus* is accomplished.

> D inflicts a wound upon P with the intent to kill him. Then, believing that he has killed P he disposes of the corpse. In fact P was not killed by the wound but dies as a result of the act of disposal. D has undoubtedly caused the *actus reus* of murder by the act of disposal, although he did not at that time have *mens rea*.

144. Ibid., 59.
145. Ibid., 64–65.

9.3 Islamic Law and *Mens Rea* (*'Amd*)

In Islamic law intention has been given due importance right from the start. The Qur'ān identified *'amd* in the offence of murder. A *mutawātir* tradition lays down the principle that "all acts are determined by intentions."[146] The Ḥanafī school does not apply this tradition as a general principle for worldly acts. Acts with respect to the Hereafter accept this general principle, but their are many exceptions for the acts of this world. In any case, the principle is applicable to some crimes. The main thing we are concerned with here are the standards used for determining intention or *mens rea.*

9.3.1 *'Amd* and its External Standards

Western law is concerned with "what goes on in the mind of the accused." For this it uses various standards including those of "probability," "foresight as to consequences," the standard of the "reasonable man." In the United States, the Model Penal Code suggests that in legislation the words "purposely," "knowingly," "recklessly," should be used as they lend themselves to a better analysis of *mens rea.* In England too the words "knowingly," "wilfully," "maliciously," "permitting," "suffering," "allowing," "causing," and "corruptly" have acquired settled meanings. The Pakistan Penal Code employs most of these words in such meanings.

Islamic law, on the other hand, follows an objective method in contracts as well as in crimes. The inner intention or "what goes on in the mind of the accused" is difficult to determine. In contracts, therefore, it goes by the objective meanings of words used in the formation of contracts and does not attempt to explore the subjective intentions of the contracting parties. In crimes, it fixes *external standards* that do or are likely to convey the inner workings of the mind of the offender.

The *external standards* have not been invented by the jurists on their own, but are based on textual evidences. The primary evi-

146. <'innamA al-'a'mAlu bi-al-nni—-yyAt>

dences on which these standards are based are traditions from the Prophet (p.b.u.h.).

The first is the tradition that distinguishes between *'amd* (intention) and *shibh al-'amd* (quasi intention). The tradition says that for the person who is killed with a stick (or a whip) *diyah* (100 camels) is to be paid. Here the use of a stick in causing death becomes an external standard that indicates that death was not intended by the offender, although the intention was to cause grievous hurt.

The second tradition says: <al-qawad bi-al-sayf> . This is interpreted in two ways. The first is that in death by *qiṣāṣ*, the offender is to be executed with the sword. The second meaning, which is more relevant here, is that homicide caused with a sword leads to *qiṣāṣ*. In other words, the use of the sword becomes an external standard for the intention to kill; the offender who was using a sword for his aggression intended to kill. *Mens rea* is, therefore, attributed to such an offender.

From the traditions, the schools of law, especially the Ḥanafī school, derived a general rule for such external standards. The rule may be stated thus: "*Mens rea* of murder is found when the offender uses an instrument *prepared* for killing." This would cover all methods and instruments that are primary intended for killing, like guns, swords, knives, arrows, poison, and lethal weapons of all kinds.

The extent to which the jurists tried to follow the texts in determining such standards, and avoiding their own subjective reasoning, is indicated by many examples and discussions in *fiqh* literature. For example, Abū Ḥanīfah following the general rule of a "weapon prepared for killing" does not include death caused with a blunt instrument within *qatl 'amd*. For this he has been criticized by other jurists. His argument is that *qiṣāṣ* is an extreme penalty and only extreme cases—of lethal weapons—should be included to define the *actus reus* of the offence of murder. Thus, a wooden club would not lead to a conviction under *qatl 'amd,* and would be *shibh al-'amd.*

The criticism against him increases when he goes ahead and includes an iron rod within the *actus reus* of murder, when an iron rod is a blunt instrument. He appears to be violating his own principle in this case, because an iron rod is not an instrument "prepared for killing." His argument is that he is not using his own mind here; as this is a very serious matter, he has to follow the texts. He replies that he is relying on the words of the Qur'ān:

وانزلنا الحديد فيه بأس شديد

We have sent down iron; in it is great strength

There can be many arguments for and against the objective standard followed by Islamic law and the more or less subjective standard followed in the law. The vital issue, however, is: are we to follow the traditions for determining such matters?

9.3.2 External standards and the law of *qiṣāṣ*

§300 of the PPC defining the *actus reus* of *qatl 'amd,* borrows the language of the earlier provision for murder for determining "what is going on in the mind of the accused." In other words, the *external standards* used by the *fuqahā'* have been avoided.

As compared to this, the definition of *shibh al-'amd* in §315 appears to mix both standards. It talks about the type of "weapon" as well as "an act which in the ordinary course of nature is not likely to cause death." The word "weapon" if it means something readied for killing is not relevant to *shibh al-'amd,* but to *qatl 'amd.* The illustration to the section says: "A in order to cause hurt strikes Z with a stick or stone which in the ordinary course of nature is not likely to cause death. Z dies as a result of such hurt. A shall be guilty of *qatl shibh-i-'amd.*" Here, then, sticks and stones are not all sticks and stones—blunt instruments, as is the meaning in the tradition, but a "stick or stone which in the ordinary course of nature is not likely to cause death." Besides being contrary to the tradition, the question is how will the court decide which stick or stone is not likely to cause death in the ordinary course of nature. In our view, the void-for-vagueness rule can easily be applied to §315.

It is suggested that we should not mix standards. Mixing standards is likely to make an already difficult area of the law more complex and perhaps confusing.

9.4 Negligence and *Mens Rea*

A person is negligent if his conduct in relation to a reasonably intelligible risk falls below the standard which would be expected of a reasonable person in the light of that risk.[147] The risk involved in the conduct may concern a consequence of such conduct or a circumstance in relation to which it occurs.[148]

It is not proper to describe negligence as *mens rea,* although writers differ about this issue. This is especially true when *mens rea* is taken in its literal meaning of a "guilty mind."[149] As the proof of negligence does not need to show "what was going on in the accused's head," it cannot be included in the meaning of *mens rea.*

It may be mentioned that there are very few crimes in English law in which negligence is the gist of the offence. In the Pakistan Penal Code too the offences requiring proof of negligence are few. The most important examples are those of: §319—*qatl-i-khata* by rash or negligent act; §320—death by rash and negligent driving; §337-G—hurt by rash or negligent driving; §337-H—hurt by rash or negligent act. A few other sections are mentioned below.

9.4.1 Negligence as non-compliance with an objective standard

Intention, recklessness and negligence all involve a failure to comply with an objective standard of conduct.[150] In intention and even in recklessness a *state of mind* must be proved. This state of mind requires the judge to discover "what goes on in the mind of the accused," as discussed in the last section in the previous chapter. Negligence, on the other hand, may be conclusively proved by simply showing that D's conduct failed to measure up to an objective standard. It is not necessary to prove that D did not forsee

147. Cross and Jones, *Introcuction to Criminal Law,* 47.
148. Ibid.
149. Smith and Hogan, *Criminal Law,* 82.
150. Ibid., 81.

the risk, ie, he had no knowledge of it or the idea did not cross his mind.

Negligence is *conduct* which departs from the standard to be expected of a reasonable man.[151] The standard by which negligence is judged may be considered in two forms on the basis of the conduct of the accused:

1. **Where no specialized knowledge was involved in the conduct.** For this type of conduct no state of mind need be proved.

2. **Where specialized knowledge is involved.** When the accused has specialized knowledge which the ordinary person would not possess, the issue to be settled is whether a reasonable man possessed with that knowledge would have acted as he did. In this case the state of mind becomes relevant. Behaviour with a revolver, which is not negligent in the case of an ordinary person with no specialized knowledge might be grossly negligent if committed by a firearms expert.[152] This type of standard may be expected of a public servant who negligently suffers a person to escape from custody under §223 PPC. §269 of the PPC reads:

    > Whoever lawfully or negligently does any act which is, and which he knows or has reason to believe to be, likely to spread the infection of any disease dangerous to life, shall be punished with imprisonment of either description for a term which may extend to six months or with fine, or with both.

    Here a state of mind is also required to proved, because of the words "which he knows or has reason to believe to be."[153] This shows that in cases of negligence a higher standard is expected of a person with specialized knowledge and greater foresight.

---

151. Ibid.
152. Ibid.
153. *Cf.* §§284–289 PPC.

9.4.2 Negligence and Islamic law

Islamic law treats negligence as part of *khata'*, which is a generic term that includes cases of unintended consequences where their was intention to cause harm, negligence, as well as strict liability. The reason is that the penalty provided for in all these cases is the same—*diyah*, or some other form of compensation. As the *fuqahā'* are dealing with the rights of the individuals under this category, they do not feel the need to provide further penalties.

If the sate wishes to deal with negligence specifically, it may do so under its *siyāsah* jurisdiction pursuing the rights of the state. This is exactly what has been done under the provisions of the law of *qiṣāṣ* and *diyah* now incorporated in the PPC. For example, §319 provides as follows:

> *Punishment for qatl-i-khata.*—Whoever commits *qatl-i-khata* shall be liable to *diyat:*
>
> Provided that, where *qatl-i-khata* is committed by any rash or negligent act, other than rash or negligent driving, the offender may, in addition to *diyat*, also be punished with imprisonment of either description for a term which may extend to five years as *ta'zīr*.

Here the state exercising its right has provided an additional penalty of 5 years imprisonment as *ta'zīr*.

9.4.2.1 Should negligence be a basis for liability

We have said that traditional Islamic law does not feel the necessity of considering negligence as part of the bases of liability. Many voices have been raised against this concept in modern law as well. These writers contend that negligence should have no place in criminal liability. We may note two of these arguments here, both have been provided by Jerome Hall, one of the greatest legal minds of this century:[154]

- **Punishment does not deter negligence.** Providing penalties for negligence is not in accordance with the purposes of

154. Jerome Hall, *General Principles of Criminal Law*, 136.

the criminal law, ie, deterrence. Hall rejects the view that punishment stimulates care, arguing that the deterrent theory postulates a man who weighs the possibility of punishment in the balance before acting; but the inadvertent harm-doer, by definition does not do this. In other words, negligence is the result of conduct that could not be helped by the accused and the test of "foresight" cannot be applied here. This is especially true when penalties are being provided on the basis of recklessness (or rashness according to the PPC) as well as on the basis of strict liability.

- **Negligently caused harm does not represent moral fault.** Hall contends that it is difficult to accept that negligently caused harm reflects a moral fault. He rejects the thesis that negligent persons may be ethically blameworthy insofar as they are insensitive to the rights of others.

The solution provided by Islamic law in such cases is to provide compensation to the victim.

Discussion Questions

1. What are the elements of crime and what is their nature?
2. Describe the meaning of *actus reus* and identify its elements.
3. What rules have been laid down for the *actus reus*? Elaborate these rules with the help of illustrations.
4. What are the implications of the statement that the criminal act must be voluntary?
5. Distinguish between specific intent and general intent with enumeration of crimes for each.
6. What is transferred malice? Explain with the help of illustrations. Does Islamic law acknowledge it?
7. When is omission treated as a criminal act?
8. What is the difference between intention and recklessness?
9. What do you understand by basic *mens rea*?
10. Distinguish between intention and motive. How is motive relevant in a criminal proceeding?

11. Why is concurrence between *mens rea* and the *actus reus* essential for criminal liability, and what does it mean?
12. Islamic law uses external standards for determining *mens rea*? Comment.
13. Would it be correct to say that Islamic law focuses on the *actus reus* alone and does not consider *mens rea* as a separate element? Argue for and against such a method.
14. Compare the standards used in Islamic law with those of Western law for determining *mens rea.*

CHAPTER 10

STRICT LIABILITY OFFENCES

The most absurd apology for authority and law is that they serve to diminish crime. Aside from the fact that the State is itself the greatest criminal, breaking every written and natural law, stealing in the form of taxes, killing in the form of war and capital punishment, it has come to an absolute standstill in coping with crime. It has failed utterly to destroy or even minimize the horrible scourge of its own creation.

Emma Goldman,
Anarchism

We are now in a position to classify offences according to those that require proof of intention, recklessness and negligence. Crimes which do not require intention, recklessness or even negligence as to one or more elements in the *actus reus* are known as offences of strict liability.[155] Offences may, therefore, be classified as in the figure below. In this chapter, we shall discuss strict liability and compare its meaning, as far as possible, with vicarious liability.

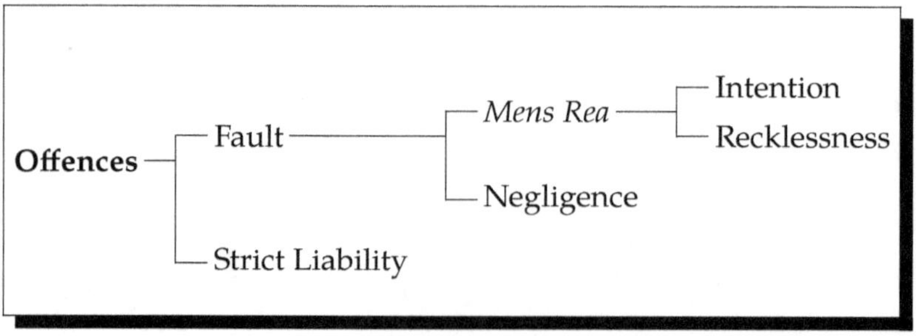

155. Smith and Hogan, *Criminal Law,* 873.

10.1 The meaning of strict liability

A strict liability offence is one that does not require awareness of all of the factors constituting the crime. Generally, the requirement of a state of mind is not abandoned with respect to all elements of the offence, but only with regard to one or some. The major significance of an offence's being a strict liability offence is that certain defences, such as mistake of fact are not available.

Strict liability offences are sometimes referred to as "absolute prohibition" offences, but this term is misleading if not incorrect. For the reason we have to recall the meaning of *actus reus*, which is something that is made up of a *number of elements*. Absolute prohibition implies that *mens rea* need not be proved for all these elements. On the other hand, if an offence has been defined in such a way that *mens rea* is not required for even a single element of the *actus reus*, the offence is one of strict liability. The single element that does not require *mens rea* will usually be one of great significance. Thus, on a charge of selling meat unfit for human consumption, it may not be necessary to prove that the defendant knew that the meat was unfit for consumption. This does not mean that proof of *mens rea* will not be required for showing that the defendant *indeed intended to sell* the meat.

10.2 Strict liability at common law

The general rule at Common law was that there were no strict liability offences. The following offences are said to be exceptions to this rule:

1. **Public nuisance:** A master may be held liable for the act of his servant even though he himself did not know it had taken place. This, in fact, is an offence of vicarious liability and not one of strict liability.

2. **Criminal libel:** A publisher could be held liable for criminal libel on the part of his employee. This was changed by the Libel Act of 1843, which provided that it is a valid defence to show that the publication was without his authority.

3. **Contempt of court:** It is an offence to publish inaccurate reports of evidence at trial in such a manner that the members of the jury might be influenced in their decision. This has been affirmed by the Contempt of Court Act 1981.

4. **Blasphemy:** A writing is blasphemous when it has a *tendency* to shock and outrage Christians. It is not necessary to prove that the defendant was aware of this tendency. It is sufficient to show that he *intentionally used* words which, in fact, are likely to shock and outrage.

10.3 Examples of strict liability offences in Pakistan

In Pakistan, most of the strict liability offences are to be found in the following areas.

1. Blasphemy
2. Drugs
3. *Qatl khata'* and unintended injuries where compensation in some form has to be paid.
4. Weapons
5. Driving and Traffic Offences

10.4 Recognition of strict liability offences

Strict liability offences, also known as public welfare offences, are generally "regulatory" offences, i.e., offences that are part of a regulatory scheme. They generally involve a relatively low penalty and are not regarded by the community as involving significant moral impropriety. The mere fact, however, that a statute is silent on the question of mental state does not necessarily mean that the offence is a strict liability offence. If no mental state is expressly required by the statute, the courts may still interpret the statute as requiring some *mens rea, especially if the statute imposes a severe penalty*. In Pakistan, the liability for some strict liability offences is death.

The definition of a strict liability offence usually does not include the word "knowingly." Where the word "knowingly" is used *mens rea* as to all the elements of the *actus reus* is usually required.

10.5 Why is strict liability imposed?

A number of arguments are advanced for and against strict liability. The arguments given in favour are:

1. **The primary function of courts is the prevention of crime and strict liability deals with this most effectively.** Criminologists like Barbara Wootton have strongly supported this reason.

2. **Without it guilty people would escape punishment.** The argument is advanced that there is neither the time nor the personnel available to litigate the culpability of each particular infraction. The argument assumes that it is possible to deal with these cases without deciding whether or not the defendant had *mens rea,* and whether or not he was negligent.

3. **It is necessary to impose strict liability in the public interest.** In many of the instances in which strict liability has been imposed, the public does need protection against negligence. The greater the degree of social danger, the more likely the imposition of strict liability. Inflation, drugs, road accidents and pollution are constantly brought to our attention as pressing evils, and in each of these cases strict liability is imposed in the interest of the public and the protection of society. Strict liability has, however, been been imposed mostly in three types of cases:

   a) Acts which are "not criminal in any real sense" but are prohibited in the public interest under a penalty.

b) Public nuisances.

c) Proceedings which though criminal in form are really only a means of enforcing a civil right.

10.6 Strict liability and Islamic law

In Islamic law, the general rule of proving intention is strictly followed. Strict liability is against the general rule that "acts are to be determined in the light of intentions." It is for this reason that strict liability has been used in a limited way and usually for the reason at 3(c) mentioned above, ie, "proceedings which though criminal in form are really only a means of enforcing a civil right."

Thus, cases of *khata* may be treated as those of strict liability. Compensation has to be paid to the heirs of the victim. The same is true in the case of destruction of property. This rule, however, is applied so strictly that even minors and lunatics are held to be financially liable, even though they lack capacity and hence *mens rea*.

It is, therefore, suggested that in the light of Islamic law strict liability may be used:

1. When proceedings which though criminal in form are really only a means of paying damages of compensation (*ḍamān*).

2. In the public interest when there is social danger. In such cases, the punishment to be awarded should not exceed one year of simple imprisonment. Wherever, the punishment is more than one year's imprisonment, the requirement of *mens rea*, intention or recklessness, should be made mandatory. If the statute fails to mention *mens rea* in the case of heavy penalties, the courts should interpret it to be included in the definition.

Discussion Questions

1. What is strict liability and what is its relationship with *mens rea* and negligence?

2. How many strict liability offences can you identify for the law in Pakistan?
3. Give reasons why the criminal law imposes strict liability.
4. How does Islamic law deal with strict liability?

CHAPTER 11

PARTIES TO CRIMES AND INCHOATE OFFENCES

Order derived through submission and maintained by terror is not much of a safe guaranty; yet that is the only "order" that governments have ever maintained. True social harmony grows naturally out of solidarity of interests. In a society where those who always work never have anything, while those who never work enjoy everything, solidarity of interests is non-existent; hence social harmony is but a myth.... Thus the entire arsenal of governments—laws, police, soldiers, the courts, legislatures, prisons—is strenuously engaged in "harmonizing" the most antagonistic elements in society.

Emma Goldman,
Anarchism

11.1 Accomplice Liability at Common Law

The common law distinguished four types of parties to a felony:[156]

156. At common law, these distinctions between the parties had a great deal of procedural significance. For example, an accessory could not be convicted unless the principal had already been convicted, although both could be convicted in a joint trial if the jury determined the principal's guilt first. Some of these distinctions have now been abandoned. Thus, in some jurisdictions in the United States, an accessory can be convicted even if the principal has evaded apprehension or has been tried and acquitted. Most jurisdictions in that country have also abolished the distinctions between principals in the first degree and principals in the second degree or accessories before the fact (assessories after the fact are still treated separately). Under the modern approach, all "parties to the crime" can be found guilty of the criminal offence.

1. **principals in the first degree** (persons who actually engage in the act or omission that constitutes the criminal offence);
2. **principals in the second degree** (persons who aid, command, or encourage the principal **and are present at the crime**);
3. **accessories before the fact** (persons who aid, abet or encourage the principal **but are not present at the crime**);
4. **accessories after the fact** (persons who assist after the crime).

11.2 Understanding Important Concepts

To understand the meaning of abetment it is necessary to examine some basic terms in the light of the above categories. Some of these terms have not been used in the Pakistan Penal Code, but they clarify the concepts.

1. **Principal or Perpetrator:** Today, when we talk of a principal or perpetrator, we are combining the first two categories out of the four mentioned for the common law above, ie, principal in the first dgree and principal in the second degree. Both are present at the crime. Thus, a perpetrator, otherwise known as a principal, may be classified as follows:

    a) A principal is one who, with the requisite mental state, actually engages in the act or omission that causes the criminal result. He is the person whose act has a causal link with the *actus reus*.

    b) A principal is anyone who acts through an innocent, irresponsible, or unwilling agent to cause the criminal result. Thus, if a A gives some powder to her daughter so that she may give it to B, her father (A's husband), to cure his cold, and the powder turns out to be poison, A is a perpetrator and the daughter an innocent agent. This is true if the daughter was unaware that the powder contained poison. This is the position under English law. §108 of the PPC, however, calls such a perpetrator an abettor. Illustration (b) to Explanation 3 of the section is as follows:

> A, with intention of murdering Z, instigates B, a child under seven years of age, to do an act which causes Z's death. B in consequence of the abetment, does the act in the absence of A, and thereby, causes Z's death. Here, though B was not capable by law of committing an offence, A is liable to be punished in the same manner as if B had been capable by law of committing an offence, and had committed murder, and he is therefore subject to the punishment of death.

Islamic law, in such a case, considers the innocent agent to be a "mere instrument" in the hands of the person acting through such agent. In other words, the offender will be charged as a perpetrator or principal and not an abettor.

In the above illustration A was not present. What if he had been when B committed the act that caused death? The next category provides the answer.

c) A person who is otherwise an abettor of an offence becomes a perpetrator when he is present at the crime, even if he did not engage in the commission of the act himself, ie, actually bring about the *actus reus* himself. Under the common law categories mentioned above, such a person was called principal in the second degree. §114 of the Pakistan Penal Code states:

> Whenever any person, who if absent would be liable to be punished as an abettor, is present when the act or offence for which he would be punishable in consequence of the abetment is committed, he shall be deemed to have committed such act or offence.

Thus, he will be charged as a principal or perpetrator and not as an abettor, because he was present at the crime.

2. **Abettor:** An abettor under the four common law categories would be an accessory before the fact. In Enlgish law, however, fine distinctions are drawn between "aiding," "abetting," "encouraging," and "procuring." The general term used for all these categories is "accomplice," which coincides with an accessory before the fact who is not present at the crime. The Pakistan Penal Code appears to use the term "abettor," in a very wide sense as it includes the common law offences of instigation or incitement as well as conspiracy, besides "aiding" in the sense of the English term "accomplice."[157] From a reading of §114 alongwith §§107 and 108, it appears that an abettor is a person who is not present at the crime. This is strengthened by the fact that the distinction is maintained very strictly in the case of a person acting through an innocent agent, where he is considered an abettor if he is not present at the crime. This has been discussed above. The distinction gets blurred though when one examines certain cases falling under instigation and conspiracy. In addition, the meaning of the words "at the time of commission of an act" in *Explanation 2* to §107 would imply that the abettor is present at the crime. The main issue would be of the offence under which the offender is charged.

3. **Accessory after the fact:** An accessory after the fact is one who receives, relieves, comforts, or assists another knowing that he has committed a felony, in order to help the felon escape arrest, trial, or conviction. The crime committed by the principal must be a felony and it must be completed at the time the aid is rendered. Today, the crime is usually called "harbouring an offender," "aiding escape," or "obstructing justice." §§212–216-A, alongwith others, are examples of such offences (under the chapter "Of False Evidence and Offences Against Justice")

157. An accomplice is one who aids, counsels, or encourages the principal before or during the commission of the crime.

11.3 Criminal Conspiracy

11.3.1 Meaning of Criminal Conspiracy

At common law, conspiracy was defined as "an agreement to do an unlawful act or lawful act by unlawful means"[158] This definition was incorporated in §120-A, which was inserted in the PPC by an amendement of 1913. §120-A defines criminal conspiracy as follows:

> When two or more persons agree to do, or cause to be done,—
>
> (1) an illegal act, or
>
> (2) an act which is not illegal by illegal means,
>
> such an agreement is designated a criminal conspiracy:

11.3.2 Object of Criminal Conspiracy: Illegal Act

It is crucial to note that the object of the offence of criminal conspiracy, as defined in § 120A, is not "an offence," but an "illegal act." In earlier times in the common law, the illegal act or unlawful act was interpreted widely to mean two things:

1. *Offence as illegal act:* This is any act that is defined as an offence in the PPC. The explanation to §120 states that "it is immaterial whether the illegal act is the ultimate object of such agreement, or is merely incidental to that object."

2. *Illegal act that is not an offence:* In England, the term "unlawful" or "illegal" act for purposes of criminal conspiracy was defined in a very broad sense and included some torts as well.[159] Thus, an agreement to commit a tort will also amount to criminal conspiracy. It is for this reason

158. Lord Denman in *Jones* (1832) 4 B & Ad 345 at 349, as quoted in Ormerod, *Simth and Hogan: Criminal Law*, 359.
159. ibid.,

that §120A says: " Provided that no agreement 'except an agreement to commit an offence' shall amount to a criminal conspiracy unless some act besides the agreement is done by one or more parties to such agreement in pursuance thereof." Here the section is saying that when the object of the agreement is not an offence, some additional act would be required for it to amount to criminal conspiracy. It is not clear what this additional act should be.

3. **Illegal means for a legal act:** The act may in itself be legal, but the means adopted to achieve it may be illegal, and such means it is implied, may be offences in themselves or other illegal acts like torts.

In Englad, the Law Commission has pursued the objective that criminal conspiracy should be confined to agreements to commit offences.[160]

11.3.3 Essential Ingredients of Criminal Conspiracy

In the light of §120-A and common law concepts, the following essential ingredients may be derived:

1. **There must be an intention to form an agreement: *mens rea*:** Ormerod maintains that it is very difficult to separate *mens rea* from the *actus reus*, because the agreement itself is a mental act. Nevertheless, the following are considered the *mens rea* in this offence: (1) and intention to agree; (2) an intention to carry out the agreement; and (3) intention or knowledge of circumstances forming part of the illegal act.

2. **There must be an agreement must be to undertake an "illegal act" or a "legal act" by unlawful means: *actus reus*:** The actus reus of the offence of criminal conspiracy is the agreement itself where the object of the agreement is an offence. Where it is not an offence, but another illegal act, another act is required to complete the actus reus.

160. Ibid., 360.

11.3.4 Punishment for Criminal Conspiracy

§120B lays down punishments for the offence of criminal conspiracy as follows:

1. **Conspiracy to commit an offence:** Where the criminal conspiracy is to commit an offence punishable with death, imprisonment for life or rigorous imprisonment for a term of two years or upwards, and no express provision is made in the PPC for the punishment of such a conspiracy, the punishment will be provided as if the offender had abetted such offence.

2. **Conspiracy to commit an act that is not offence:** Where the criminal conspiracy is to commit an act that is not an offence, the punishment will be up to six months imprisonment.

11.4 Abetment of an Offence

According to §107, a person abets the doing of a thing in three ways:

1. **By Instigation:** A person abets the doing of a thing, who instigates any person to do that thing. *Explanation 1* to §107 says: A person who, by wilful misrepresentation, or by wilful concealment of a material fact, which he is bound to disclose, volunarily causes or procures, or attempts to cause or procure, a thing to be done, is said to instigate the doing of that thing." The illustration to this section is as follows:

   > A, a public officer, is authorized by a warrant from a Court of Justice to apprehend Z. B, knowing the fact and also that C is not Z, wilfully represents to A that C is Z, and thereby intentionally causes A to apprehend C. Here B abets by instigation the apprehension of C.

   Abetment by instigation coincides with the offence of "incitement" under the English law, which was established in the case of *Higgins* (1801). In the United States the word "solicitation" is preferred. The main similarity between the common law offence of "incitement" and instigation is that both are complete offences. This is strengthened by the meaning of instigation provided in *Explanation 1* where even "attempts to cause or procure" have been deemed instigation. **It is, perhaps, for this reason that the PPC did not feel the need to define instigation or incitement as a separate substantive offence,** unlike conspiracy which we consider next.

2. **Abetment by conspiracy:** See the meaning of conpiracy above.

   "A person abets the doing of a thing, who ...[e]ngages with one or more other person or persons in any conspiracy for the doing of that thing, if an act or illegal omission takes place in pursuance of that conspiracy, and in order to the doing of that thing." The words "if an act or illegal omission takes place in pursuance of that conspiracy" are to be noted here. **They imply that abetment by conspiracy is not a complete offence. It becomes punishable when the act committed is actually brought about.** It was for this reason that the common law offence of "criminal conspiracy" was defined separately as a "complete offence" by the addition of Chapter V-A, §§120-A and 120-B, in 1913. As regards the punishment for criminal conspiracy, §120-B says that the offender shall "be punished in the same manner as if he had abetted such an offence." The details of the offence of criminal conspiracy cannot be discussed here, however, the main thing to be noticed is that:

   a) there has to be an agreement;
   b) conspiracy has to be committed by two or more persons, as an agreement cannot be conceived through the act of a single person; instigation and aiding on the other hand are possible by the act of one person.

3. **Abetment by aiding:** A person abets the doing of a thing, who intentionally aids, by an act or illegal omission, the do-

ing of that thing. *Explanation 2* to §108 states that "[w]hoever, either prior to or at the time of commission of an act, does anything in order to facilitate the commission of that act, and thereby facilitates the commission thereof, is said to aid the doing of that act." **The words "at the time of commission of an act" imply that the abettor may be present at the crime.** For example, A hands over a cup of poison to B who is committing suicide. Here A intentionally aids B in the commission of an offence.

11.5 Who is an Abettor?

§108 defines an abettor as follows:

> A person abets an offence, who abets either the commission of an offence, or the commission of an act which would be an offence, if committed by a person capable by law of committing an offence with the same intention or knowledge, as that of the abettor.

An abettor is a person who abets the commission of an offence through two types of persons:

1. A person capable of forming an intention for the offence. In this case abetment is possible through all the methods of abetment described under §107, ie, instigation, conspiracy and aiding.

2. An "innocent agent" who cannot form an intention and thus is not capable of committing the offence with the same knowledge and intention as that of the abettor. The explanation of the meaning of an "innocent agent" has preceded above. This would also exclude the case of abetment by conspiracy, as the innocent agent may not be able to give his consent for the agreement necessary for the conspiracy.

In addition to this, the following conditions are to be noted:

1. Abetment is possible through abetment of an illegal omission by the person abetted. The abettor may not be under a legal obligation to perform such an act. (§108, *Explanation 1*)

2. It is not necessary that the offence abetted should be committed, or the effect desired through abetment be caused. (§108, *Explanation 2*). This explanation states that abetment is a complete offence even if the result desired by the abettor, or any result in consequence of the abetment, is not achieved. **The exception to this condition,** as noted above, arises in the case of abetment through conspiracy where it is specifically mentioned that an act or omission must take place "in pursuance of that conspiracy."

11.6 Inchoate Offences

11.6.1 The Meaning of Inchoate Offences

The word inchoate does not imply that the offences are incomplete. An inchoate offence is committed prior to and in preparation for what may be a more serious offence. It is a complete offence in itself, even though the act to be done may not have been completed.

At common law there were three inchoate offences: incitement, conspiracy and attempt. As indicated above, the offence of instigation or incitement has been made part of the generic offence of abetment. Abetment through instigation being a complete offence in itself, the Pakistan Penal Code does not define it separately. As against this, the offence of abetment by way of conspiracy is not a complete offence and is dependent on the occurrence of the offence "in pursuance of the conspiracy." In 1913, a need was felt to bring this offence in line with the common law concept of a complete offence and new sections were added, as explained above. Attempt was also a complete offence at common law.

11.6.2 Attempt

The Pakistan Penal Code does not define attempt in the abstract sense, and its meaning has been left to be understood within the crimes where attempt has been made punishable. §511, the last section in the code, makes attempt punishable in a general way.

A criminal attempt is an act that, although done with the intention of committing a crime, for one reason or another falls short of completing the crime. An attempt therefore consists of two elements:

1. **A specific intent to commit the crime.** The defendant must have the intent to perform an act and obtain a result that, if achieved, would constitute a crime. Regardless of the intent required for a completed offence, an attempt always requires a specific intent. For example, attempted murder requires the specific intent to kill another person, even though the mens rea for murder itself does not require a specific intent. A crime defined as the negligent production of a result cannot be attempted, because if there were an intent to cause such a result, the appropriate offence would be attempt to intentionally commit the crime rather than attempt to negligently cause the harm. Although a strict liability crime does not require criminal intent, to attempt a strict liability crime the defendant must act with the intent to bring about the proscribed result.

2. **An overt act in furtherance of that intent.** The defendant must have committed an act beyond mere preparation for the offence. In common law countries, courts have devised several tests to determine whether the act requirement for attempt liability has been satisfied. In America, for example, there are tests called the proximity test and the equivocality test. Under the typical proximity test, attempt requires an act that is dangerously close to success. Under the equivocality test the act by itself must demonstrate that the defendant had an unequivocal intent to commit the crime.

The matters pertaining to defences employed in attempt cases and issues of abandonment and penalties provided are to be studied within the specific offences.

11.6.3 Islamic law, Abetment, and Attempt

The offences of abetment (in all its forms) and attempt can be justified on the basis of the doctrine of *siyāsah shar'īyah* in a general way for awarding *ta'zīr* penalties. In certain cases, like conspiracy, some direct evidence can be found in the textual evidences. This does not mean, however, that the state of the law as found in the Pakistan Penal Code is free from defects; it is not.

The main objection to the provisions of abetment and conspiracy is that they contradict a fundamental aim and legal principle of the criminal law. The law as stated is too technical for the common man to understand. The basic principle of the law alluded to maintains that it is the aim of the criminal law "to give fair warning of the nature of the conduct declared to be an offence." (see page 70) This is supported by the following verse of the Qur'ān:

وما كنّا معذّبين حتّى نبعث رسولا

> Nor would We visit with our wrath until we had sent a messenger (to give warning).[161]

The verse implies that no punishment is to be awarded, unless the conduct that amounts to an offence has been clearly elaborated and announced. The truth is that even those trained in the law sometimes fail to understand the technicalities of accomplice liability. The result of such vague laws is that the ordinary citizen is often placed in a precarious position, as the law can be misused by those bent upon doing so. This is not the case in Pakistan alone, but also in England. It is for this reason that reform has been recommended in England to simplify and streamline the law dealing with this area. An excerpt from a well known book discussing a report on criminal law reform is reproduced below.

161. Qur'ān 17 : 15

> The brief outline of the law given above discloses the technicalities involved in the law of complicity and the difficulties which it can produce.
>
> These difficulties have led to the interesting suggestion that the law governing complicity should cease to treat the accomplice as party to the offence which he assists or encourages, and that there should be a general and separate offence of aiding or encouraging crime. In addition to direct acts of encouragement, it should include the doing of acts known to be likely to assist the commission of an offence by another. The fact that the other would or did fail to commit an offence because of insanity, duress etc should be immaterial. Anyone who has had to contend with the technicalities of the law of complicity must surely hope that the most serious consideration be given to the suggestion when the proposed criminal code is drafted. It is unfortunate that the Law Commission Working Paper on the subject of complicity did not discuss this suggestion but proposed in essence that the law should be codified very much as it is now, subject to the clarification or reform of certain matters.[162]

The last sentence of the passage has a familiar ring to it.

Discussion Questions

1. List the rules of accomplice liability at common law and highlight the important concepts associated with it.
2. How does the Pakistani law differ from the common law of accomplice liability?
3. What are the various ways in which the offence of abetment may take place under the Pakistan Penal Code?
4. What is the difference between abetment through conspiracy and the offence of criminal conspiracy under the PPC?
5. What is the liability of an abettor acting through an "innocent agent"—at common law and under the PPC?
6. Who is the abettor under the PPC?

162. Cross and Jones, *Introduction to Criminal Law,* 462 (Footnotes omitted).

7. What do you understand by the term inchoate offences?
8. What is the meaning of attempt under the PPC? What is the relationship between attempt and strict liability offences?
9. How does Islamic law deal with abetment, conspiracy and attempt?
10. Do you think that the law of abetment as it stands today is too technical and beyond the comprehension of the common man?

CHAPTER 12

CAPACITY

Good lawyers know the law; great lawyers know the judge.

Author Unknown

12.1 Infancy

12.1.1 Presumptions at common law

An infant in England is anyone under the age of 18 years. At common law, the defence of lack of capacity to commit a crime by reason of infancy gave rise to three presumptions. All three presumptions were governed by the physical age at the time of the crime not at the time of the trial. The presumptions were as follows:

1. **No Criminal Liability Under the Age of Seven.** Under the age of seven, a child could not be held responsible for any crime. This was a conclusive presumption of incapability of knowing wrongfulness of acts. The rule is usually stated as the conclusive presumption that the child is *doli incapax*. It is for this reason that a person who abets, by instigation, a child to commit a crime is considered a principal. We have noted that the PPC does not follow this rule and considers the person an abettor.

2. **Rebuttable Presumption of No Criminal Liability Under the Age of Fourteen.** Children between the ages of 7 and 14 were presumed incapable of knowing the wrongfulness of their acts, but this presumption was rebuttable by clear proof in the particular case that the defendant appreciated the nature and quality of his act, e.g., conduct undertaken to

conceal the crime. Children under 14 were, however, conclusively presumed incapable of committing rape.

3. **Over Fourteen–Adult.** Children aged 14 or older were treated as adults and beyond this age a young person was considered to be "responsible for his actions entirely as if he were forty."

12.1.2 Pakistan and common law countries

In England, the age below which a child is *doli incapax* has been raised from seven to ten years. The Ingleby Committee had recommended that this age be raised to twelve years. In the United States, a number of modern statutes have abolished the presumptions of the common law and have provided that no child can be convicted of a crime until a stated age is reached, usually 13 or 14. Other states, however, retain the common law rule.

The Pakistan Penal Code declares that nothing is an offence that is done by a child under seven years of age (§82). This is the same as the common law presumption stated above. A child above the age of seven years and under twelve years of age (14 for the common law) can commit an offence, under the PPC, if such child has "sufficient maturity of understanding" to judge the nature and consequences of his act(§83). Mental maturity influences the court in the fixation of penalty.

The Railways Act, 1890, §30, lays down that if a minor under the age of twelve is involved in maliciously wrecking or attempting to wreck a train or in hurting or attempting to hurt person travelling by train, he shall be guilty of having committed the offence as an adult person. This severe provision is designed to deal with terrorist activity and appears ludicrous in the present times as far as the child is concerned.

12.1.3 Infancy and Islamic law

The rules stated above are the law that the British made for their colony. We may now look at the Islamic provisions that have been made applicable in Pakistan. After examining this position, we shall attempt to state the position in traditional Islamic law.

12.1.3.1 As applied in Pakistan

Under the new §299 of the PPC, an "adult" is a person who has attained the age of eighteen years and a "minor" is a person who is not an adult. A minor is not subject to the penalty of *qiṣāṣ* (retaliation by way of death or amputation of limb prescribed by Islamic law). If such a minor has attained sufficient maturity, he may be sentenced to imprisonment up to a period of fourteen years. The child who can have criminal responsibility under this law, then, is a minor who has attained maturity of understanding, and his age may extend from seven to eighteen years. Such a child will not be awarded the death penalty.

The *hudūd* laws provide two types of penalties. The first type is the *ḥadd* penalty, which is a fixed penalty provided by the texts of the Qur'ān and the *Sunnah.* The penalties under this type range from stoning to death to cutting of the hand, the cutting of the hand and the foot, and to flogging, the minimum being eighty stripes. The *ḥadd* penalty is not to be awarded to a child, where a child means either a person who is under the age of eighteen or a person who has not attained puberty. It is only in the case of the offence of *zinā* that a girl is a child if she is under the age of sixteen. For the purpose of these penalties, the minimum age of a child would be the age of actual puberty at the time of the commission of the offence, which has to be proved. In the case of rape liable to *ḥadd,* a minor who is fifteen years old may be awarded imprisonment up to five years, fine, as well as whipping up to thirty stripes. This provision appears to ignore puberty, and is probably based on the common law presumption about rape as regards a child. Even a female, including a female child, can commit this offence.

The second type of penalty provided by these laws is classified as *ta'zīr,* which is a penalty that is determined by the state (alongwith the definition of the offence) and is not provided for in the texts of the Qur'ān and the *Sunnah.* There is a wide range of these and other offences entailing an equally wide range of penalties.

The meaning of child for these offences is the same as that described for the PPC, that is, the question of puberty is not relevant, but mental maturity is the criterion for children above the age of 7 years. The Abolition of the Punishment of Whipping Act (Act VII of 1996) has the effect of abolishing the penalty of whipping in all *ta'zīr* offences, whatever the age of the offender. The new law affects §§10(2) and 10(3) of the Offence of Zina Ordinance, 1979 that prescribe the penalty of flogging, upto 30 stripes, for offences that do not fall under the fixed *ḥadd.* It also affects §11 of The Prohibition Order that prescribes the penalty of 30 stripes by way of *ta'zīr,* just as it affects §11 of The Qadhf Ordinance, 1979, which provides upto 40 stripes as *ta'zīr.*

Pakistan has signed the Convention on the Rights of the Child (CRC), and there is considerable pressure on the authorities to undertake law reform in this area. Accordingly, a proposed Child Offenders Act 1995, attempts to ban death penalty and whipping for children under 16.

12.1.3.2 As it exists in traditional law

Under the traditional Islamic law, there are three stages through which an individual passes with respect to his legal capacity.

1. The first stage is from birth till the attainment of discretion, which is considered to be the age of seven years. During this period, the child is assumed to lack *'aql* and discretion completely, and is ineligible for the assignment of a capacity for execution.
2. The second stage commences from the age of seven and continues up to actual puberty or the legal age of puberty, whichever is earlier. Deficient capacity for execution is normally assigned during this stage, as the individual possesses a certain amount of *'aql* and discretion.
3. The final stage commences from actual physical puberty or the legal age determined for it, whichever is earlier. On reaching this age the individual is assigned complete capacity for execution, and becomes eligible for each kind of *khiṭāb*. *Rushd* (discretion) is a condition for attaining this stage, in addition to puberty.

This third stage at which a person becomes an adult is associated with the external standard of puberty. The physical signs indicating the attainment of puberty are the commencement of ejaculation in a male and menstruation in a female. In the absence of these signs, puberty is presumed at the age of fifteen in both males and females according to the majority of the jurists, and at the age of eighteen for males and seventeen for females according to Abū Ḥanīfah.

Attaining *bulūgh* (puberty) alone is not sufficient, however. For a person to acquire complete capacity for execution, in addition to puberty, the possession of *rushd* (discrimination; maturity of actions) is stipulated as well. The *dalīl*, or legal evidence, for this is the verse of the Qur'ān:

> Make trial of orphans until they reach the age of marriage; then if ye find sound judgement in them, release their property to them; but consume it not wastefully, nor in haste against their growing up. [Qur'ān 4 : 6]

This verse lays down clearly that there are two conditions that must be fulfilled before the wealth of orphans can be handed over to them. These are *bulūgh al-nikāḥ* and *rushd*.

It is the second and third periods that are of greater concern to us here. In the second period, from the age of seven to the age of puberty, actual or presumed, if the child exhibits some mental maturity, the Ḥanafī school permits him beneficial financial transactions. Transactions that vacillate between benefit and harm may be undertaken subject to ratification by the guardian. Those transactions that reflect manifest loss, like making a gift, are not permitted even with the permission of the guardian. This rule is for financial liability. The rule is: only beneficial things are valid in the case of a minor.

In traditional Islamic law, a child who has not attained puberty alongwith *rushd* (mental maturity) HAS NO CRIMINAL LIABILITY. Yes, parents do have the right of *ta'dīb* (disciplining), but that does not mean criminal liability. The *khiṭāb jinā'ī* or the communication from the Lawgiver imposing criminal liability is not even addressed to such a child. This translates into a conclusive presumption that a child who has not attained puberty is not capable of committing a crime. Further, as punishments are something harmful, they would violate the rule that permits only beneficial things. Accordingly, the age of 7 years fixed for a child who is *doli incapax* should be raised to the age of puberty.

We now come to the third stage of legal capacity when puberty has been attained or is presumed. Actual physical puberty has to be proved not at the time of trial, but at the time of commission of the crime. This may be impossible in some cases. In the law, as applied in Pakistan, the presumed age of puberty is 15 according to the opinion of the majority. It is suggested that the presumed age of puberty be followed according to the opinion of Imām Abū Ḥanīfah. In the alternative, the period from the age of 15 to 18 (17 for girls) should be dealt with according to "care proceedings" as they are called, and no child should be sent to a jail during this period. The strictness of the action should increase as the age moves towards 18 from 15.

It is to be noted that a child is liable to pay damages and *diyah* irrespective of his age, without being subjected to criminal proceedings.

12.2 Insanity

The insanity defence exempts certain defendants because of the existence of an abnormal mental condition at the time of the crime. The various formulations differ significantly on what effects a mental illness must have had to entitle the defendant to acquittal. It is to be noted that insanity is a legal term rather than a psychiatric one. As such it is considered to be a generic term comprising many possible mental abnormalities. The cause of a defendant's mental illness or insanity is usually irrelevant in determining the legal consequences of the act.

12.2.1 The governing provision and rules

§84 of the PPC says: "Nothing is an offence which is done by a person who at the time of doing it, by reason of unsoundness of mind, is incapable of knowing the nature of the act, or that he is doing what is either wrong or contrary to law." There are two issues that relate to the question of insanity:

- insanity at the time of trial; and
- insanity at the time of the comission of the offence.

Chapter XXXIV (§§464–475) of the Criminal Procedure Code deals with lunatics and how the courts are going to try them or postpone trial till recovery. Here we will deal with the question of insanity at the time of the commission of the act.

In England, the **M'Naghten Rules** were formulated by the judges in 1843 to deal with legal insanity. Thus, a defendant may be insane in the medical sense, but he has to be subjected to the legal tests provided by these rules for a determination that he was insane when he did the act. §84 of the PPC appears to have been drafted in the light of these rules. The rules may be summarized as follows:

The traditional M'Naghten Rules provide that a defendant is entitled to acquittal if the proof establishes that:

1. A disease of the mind
2. Caused a defect of reason
3. Such that the defendant lacked the ability at the time of his actions to either
   a) Know the wrongfulness of his actions; or
   b) Understand the nature and quality of his actions.

The application of the rules does not consider the following to be cases of legal insanity:

1. **Defendant with Delusions.** If the defendant suffered from delusions (false beliefs), it is necessary to determine whether, if the facts had been as he believed them to be, his actions would have been criminal. For example, A, because of a mental illness, believed B wanted to kill him. A killed B. A is not entitled to acquittal on insanity grounds under the M'Naughten Rules?

2. **Belief that Acts Are Morally Right.** A defendant is not entitled to acquittal merely because he believes his acts are morally right, unless he has lost the capacity to recognize that they are regarded by society as wrong.

3. **Inability to Control Oneself.** Under the traditional interpretation given to the M'Naghten Rules, it is irrelevant that the defendant may have been unable to control himself and avoid committing the crime. Loss of control because of mental illness is no defence.

The M'Naghten Rules have been the subject of criticism, by doctors as well as lawyers, from the time they were formulated. It is said that the rules being based on outdated psychological views are too narrow. They are concerned only with the defects of reason and take no account of emotional or volitional factors whereas modern medical science is unwilling to divide the mind into separate compartments and to consider the intellect apart from the emotions and will. In the United States, the following further tests have been devised:

1. **Irresistible Impulse Test.** This test has been applied alongwith the M'Naghten Rules. Under the irresistible impulse test, a defendant is entitled to acquittal if the proof establishes that **because of mental illness he was unable to control his actions or to conform his conduct to the law.** Contrary to what the name irresistible impulse might imply, this inability need not come upon the defendant suddenly.

2. **Durham (or new Hampshire) Test.** Under the Durham rule, a defendant is entitled to acquittal if the proof establishes that his crime was the "product of mental disease or defect." A crime is a "product of" the disease if it would not have been committed but for the disease. In this way, the Durham test is broader than either the M'Naghten or irresistible impulse tests; it was intended primarily to give psychiatrists greater liberty to testify concerning the defendant's mental condition. In 1972 it was replaced with the A.L.I. test, but it remains the law in a few jurisdictions.

3. **American Law Institute (A.L.I.) or Model Penal Code Test.** Under this test, the defendant is entitled to acquittal if the proof shows that he suffered from a mental disease or defect and as a result **lacked substantial capacity** to either:

    a) Appreciate the criminality (wrongfulness) of his conduct; or

    b) Conform his conduct to the requirements of law.

    This test combines the M'Naghten and the irresistible impulse tests by allowing for the impairment of both cognitive and volitional capacity. Highly praised, the A.L.I. test is rapidly becoming the most popular formulation, and the prevailing trend is toward its use.

Many formulations (including the A.L.I. test) expressly exclude the psychopathic criminal–the person who repeatedly commits crimes without experiencing guilt. This is usually accomplished by defining "mental illness" so as to exclude any abnormality evidenced only by repeated antisocial conduct.

The Courts in this part of the world seem inclined to expand the M'Naghten Rules in accordance with the times. It is maintained that

> [I]f proved facts disclose that something falling even short of either legal insanity, satisfying the test laid down in M'Naghten Rules, which will negative criminal liability, or, "insane impulse," which is receiving increasing increaing jurisprudential recognition, for absolving its victim from criminal liablility...is present in the case so as to only disturb the normal balance of an individual's mind, what is proved may be sufficient to avert the death penalty.[163]

Islamic law: The general rule in Islamic law is that there is no criminal liability if at the time of commission of the crime the

163. (1975) 3 SCC 825.

ahlīyat al-adā' (legal capacity for execution) stood negated. The *manāṭ* (basis) for this capacity is *'aql* (reason). As soon as it ceases to function criminal capacity is lost. Islamic law also gives consideration to *ighmā'* (fits of fainting) and even to acts done during sleep. The loss of reason is a matter to be determined on the basis of empirical evidence. It would, therefore, appear that the ALI test is highly suited to the requirements of Islamic law.

12.2.2 Mental condition during criminal proceedings

The M'Naghten Rules laid down that

> [E]very man is presumed to be sane, and to possess a sufficient degree of reason to be responsible for his crimes, until the contrary is proved to [the jury's] satisfaction.[164]

Thus, all defendants are considered sane until shown to be of unsound mind. The Supreme Court has maintained, however, that the burden of proof on the defence is not as heavy as upon the prosecution in a criminal case.[165]

In addition to being a defence to criminal liability, the abnormal mental condition of a defendant is relevant at two other stages of the legal proceeding.

1. **Incompetency to Stand Trial.** As stated earlier, the Chapter on Lunatics in the Cr.PC governs this issue. The trial is to be postponed if the judge determines that the defendant is unable to understand the nature of the proceedings being brought against him or to undertake his defence. A finding of incompetence will suspend the criminal proceedings and invariably result in commitment until such time as the defendant regains competence.

2. **Incompetency at Time of Execution.** Under the common law, a defendant may not be executed if he is incapable of

164. 10 Cl & F at 210 as quoted in Smith and Hogan, *Criminal Law*, 177.
165. (1974) 3 SCC 299.

understanding the nature and purpose of the punishment. It has been held that

> The Courts have no power to prohibit the carrying out of a sentence of death legally passed upon an accused person on the ground either that there is some rule in the Common Law in England against the execution of an insane person sentenced to death or some theological, religious or moral objection to it. What the statute law does not prohibit or enjoin cannot be enforced by means of a writ of *mandamus* so as to set aside a duly passed sentence of a Court of justice.[166]

12.3 Vicarious Liability Offences

A vicarious liability offence is one in which a person without personal fault may nevertheless be held vicariously liable for the criminal conduct of another (usually an employee). The criminal law doctrine of vicarious liability is analogous to the tort doctrine of *respondeat superior.*

Strict liability dispenses with the *mens rea* requirement, but retains the requirement that the defendant have personally engaged in the necessary acts or omissions. Vicarious liability, on the other hand, dispenses with the personal *actus reus* requirement, but retains the need for mental fault on the part of the employee.

12.3.1 Limitation on punishment

An imposition of criminal liability for faultless conduct is contrary to the basic premise of criminal justice that crime requires fault on the part of the accused, it is claimed that imprisonment in such cases violates the basic principles of criminal law. The current trend in most countries is to limit vicarious liability to regulatory crimes and to limit punishment to fines. Examples of vicarious liability have already been mentioned above. (See page 142)

166. (1977) 1 SCC 180.

12.3.2 Implying vicarious liability from a strict liability offence

The mere fact that the underlying offence is clearly a strict liability offence should not imply a legislative intent to impose vicarious liability.

> For example, if a statute makes it a crime "for anyone to sell cigarrettes to a minor," the salesman may be strictly liable under this statute regardless of his belief that the customer was legally old enough to smoke, this statute should not be construed to impose liability on the owner of the shop who neither was present at the time the minor was sold the cigarrettes nor authorized the actions of the salesman.

12.3.3 Liability of corporations and associations

At common law, a corporation could not commit a crime because it was unable to form the necessary criminal intent. Modern statutes often provide for the liability of corporations and sometimes even unincorporated associations (e.g., partnerships). This liability is, by necessity, vicarious. Under such provisions, corporations may be held liable under the following conditions:

1. When the act was within the scope of office
2. When the requirements of the "superior agent rule" are met.

Even though the corporation cannot be convicted of a particular offence and cannot be imprisoned, the person who, in the name of the corporation, performs (or causes to be performed) the conduct that is an element of the offence is legally accountable and subject to punishment to the same extent as if the conduct were performed in his name or on his own behalf. Similarly, the fact that the corporation is liable does not prevent the conviction of the individual who committed the offence. The Companies Ordinance, 1984 follows this approach and in most cases individual director or official liable, not only in tort and contracts, but also in statutory violations amounting to an offence.

12.3.4 Corporate Manslaughter

After prolonged deliberation and different reports, especially the Law Commission report, *Reforming the Law on Involuntary Manslaughter*, in 2007, the Corporate Manslaughter and Corporate Homicide Act was passed by Parliament. The section dealing with the offence of corporate manslaughter reads as follows:[167]

> (1) An organisation to which this section applies is guilty of an offence if the way in which its activities are managed or organised—
>
> (a) causes a person's death, and
>
> (b) amounts to a gross breach of a relevant duty of care owed by the organisation to the deceased.

This offence is based on the Law Commission's new proposal about an offence of manslaughter that relies on gross negligence rather than on the unlawful act of manslaughter. Section 2 of the Act widens the scope of the offence to include other organisations. These are: (a) a corporation; (b) a department or other body listed in Schedule 1; (c) a police force; (d) a partnership, or a trade union or employers' association, that is an employer.[168]

The law in Pakistan does not need too many changes for implementation. A corporation is a "person" under the Pakistan Penal Code. The offences falling under *qatl-i-khata'* and *qatl-bis-sabab* do not need *mens rea* as they are strict liability offences. There is also no need to show breach of some duty or gross negligence. All that is needed is to prove a causal link between death and the act of the corporation through any of its employees. The defendants will be all the officers of the corporation, that is, CEO, directors and company secretary. Thus. there is no real need of amendment in the law, but the state may make a suitable addition to show that henceforth corporations will be liable under these sections.

167. Corporate Manslaughter and Corporate Homicide Act 2007 (2007 CHAPTER 19), section 1.
168. Ibid., section 2.

Review Questions

① How do the presumptions pertaining to infancy in the modern world today differ from the presumptions under the Penal Code?

② What in your opinion should be the presumptions for the defence of infancy in the light of Islamic law?

③ The M'Naghten rules for legal insanity have been improved in the Western world. What is the state of the application of these rules in Pakistan?

④ Compare the rules for vicarious liability in torts and crimes.

⑤ What kind of criminal liability is imposed on corporations? Give illustrations.

⑥ Write a detailed note on corporate manslaughter reform in Pakistan.

CHAPTER 13

GENERAL DEFENCES

Extreme justice is often injustice.

Jean Racine

A person is generally held criminally liable when he has caused an *actus reus* with the appropriate *mens rea.* But this is not always so as there are defences that may be available to the defendant. Defences are of two types: general and special. Special defences are those that are applicable to particular crimes (these will be studied in a separate volume on particular crimes). General defences are common to all crimes, and it is these that are discussed in this chapter. The majority of the general defences are covered in Chapter IV of the Pakistan Penal Code dealing with General Exceptions.

13.1 Necessity—Pressure from Physical or Natural Forces

Conduct otherwise criminal is justifiable if, as a result of pressure from natural forces, the defendant reasonably believed that the conduct was necessary to avoid harm to society exceeding the harm caused by the conduct. The test is objective; a good faith belief in the necessity of one's conduct is insufficient. Causing the death of another person to protect property is never justified. The defence of necessity is not available if the defendant is at fault in creating the situation requiring that he choose between two evils. §81 of the Pakistan Penal Code deals with necessity:

> Nothing is an offence merely by reason of its being done with the knowledge that it is likely to cause harm, if it be done without any criminal intention to cause harm, and in good faith for the purpose of preventing or avoiding other harm to person or property.

Jettisoning of cargo at sea during a violent storm, if necessary to save the lives of the crew and other people on board would not constitute criminal damage to property. On the other hand, jettisoning some members of the crew to save the cargo would never be justifiable.

As compared to necessity duress involves a human threat. Necessity invariably involves pressure from physical or natural forces.

A points a gun at B and threatens to kill B if he does not break into C's house and steal food, B does as he is told, B may raise the defence of duress. If, however, B is a starving victim of a plane crash in a desolate area and commits the same act, he has the defence of necessity.

13.1.1 Necessity and Islamic law

In Islamic law, necessity is called *iḍtirār* (*iztirār* in the Ordinance) and sometimes *ḍarūrah* (necessity). The distinction drawn above for the law between necessity and duress applies to Islamic law as well. Duress (*ikrāh*) is discussed below. We also need to distinguish necessity (*ḍarūrah*) (*zarūrat* in Urdu) from *ḥājah* (need). Need cannot make the unlawful lawful, whereas necessity can. The rule for necessity, however, is that necessity is limited to what is necessary. For example, it is the need of the Muslim states today to deal in interest (*ribā*) with financial institutions and developed countries, but this need can never make *ribā* lawful. Here, this need is not necessity. The state will not expire if it does not deal in interest. Necessity is a state where one is facing a threat of death, but it too cannot become an excuse for making things lawful on a more or less permanent basis; it is limited to the extent that is necessary. For example, if a man dying of thirst has only wine to quench his thirst, he may do so, but he cannot make a habit out of it.

13.2 Duress (Compulsion or Coercion)—A Human Threat

A person is not guilty of an offence, other than homicide and offences against the state punishable with death, if he performs an otherwise criminal act under the threat of imminent infliction of death or great bodily harm, provided that he reasonably believes death or great bodily harm will be inflicted on himself or on a member of his immediate family if he does not perform such conduct. Threats to harm any third person may also suffice to establish the defence of duress. It should be noted that an act committed under duress is termed excusable rather than justifiable. The subtle distinction stems from the fact that criminal acts performed under duress are condoned by society rather than encouraged. §94 of the PPC is explicit on these points:

> Except murder, and offences against the State punishable with death, nothing is an offence which is done by a person who is compelled to do it by threats, which, at the time of doing it, reasonably cause the apprehension that instant death to that person will otherwise be the consequence: Provided the person doing the act did not of his own accord, or from a reasonable apprehension of harm to himself short of instant death, place himself in a situation by which he became subject to such constraint.
>
> *Explanation 1.*—A person who of his own accord, or by reason of a threat of being beaten, joins a gang of dacoits, knowing their character, is not entitled to the benefit of this exception, on the ground of his having been compelled by his associates to do anything that is an offence by law.
>
> *Explanation 2.*—A person seized by a gang of dacoits, and forced by threat of instant death, to do a thing which is an offence by law; for example, a smith compelled to take his tools and to force the door of a house for the dacoits to enter and plunder it, is entitled to the benefit of this exception.

13.2.1 Coercion and duress (*ikrāh*) in Islamic law

13.2.1.1 Traditional Islamic law

Ikrāh is a situation in which one is forced to do something without his willingness.[169] The jurists disagree about the extent to which

169. For the details see Ṣadr al-Sharī'ah, *al-Tawḍīḥ*, vol. 2, 820.

ikrāh can affect free will. The views of these jurists may be classified into two opinions:

1. The first opinion maintains that *ikrāh* is an obstacle in the way of *taklīf* (creation of an obligation). Thus, the *khiṭāb* is not directed toward a person under coercion or under duress, because this person is prevented from understanding the *khiṭāb*. Among those who hold this opinion are Shāfi'ī jurists, who maintain that free will is a condition of *taklīf*. *Ikrāh*, according to the Shāfi'īs, arises under a threat of death, hurt, perpetual confinement, and the like. It does not arise for causes of a lesser gravity, like a threat to property.
2. The second opinion is held by the Ḥanafīs, who divide *ikrāh* into three types:

    a. First is coercion that negates free will or choice. This is coercion under threat of death or loss of limb.
    b. The second type is coercion that negates consent, but makes free will irregular or *fāsid*. This is brought about by confinement for a long period or by beating and torture that does not lead to loss of life or limb.
    c. The third type is *ikrāh* that does not negate consent nor does it make free will *fāsid*. The example is confinement of close relatives. Some Ḥanafī jurists do not accept this third category, and link it with one of the categories above, depending upon the nature of the threat to dear ones.

The Ḥanafīs maintain that the condition of *taklīf* is the existence of the right to choose and not its validity (*ṣiḥḥah*). Irregular or *fāsid* free will, they say, is sufficient for the existence of *taklīf*. In all the above cases of *ikrāh*, free will is not invalid (*bāṭil*) though it may be irregular. *Taklīf*, therefore, may accompany *ikrāh*. Acts, for this purpose, are divided into two kinds by the Ḥanafī jurists.

a. First is the case when the coerced is a mere instrument in the hands of another, like a person picking up another and throwing him upon another thereby causing death, or hurt, or causing damage to property. If A causes B to fire at a bush knowing that C is hiding behind it, thus, causing the death of C, then, A shall be guilty of murder, while B will be an instrument in his hand. Other cases can be imagined. In such cases the act is attributed not to the instrument, but to one who caused him to move.

b. Second is the case when the coerced cannot become an instrument in the hands of another, for example, in the commission of *zinā* or eating of food. In such a case, the person coerced is fully aware of his actions. Here the person coerced is guilty of *zinā* or for compensating property consumed. In the case of drinking of *khamr*, however, *ḥadd* is waived on grounds of *shubhah*.

13.2.1.2 As applied in Pakistan

The Pakistan Penal Code, in §299, now provides a definition for duress, by dividing it into two types as follows:

1. *"ikrah-e-tam"* (إکراہ تام) means putting any person, his spouse or of his blood relations within the prohibited degree of marriage in fear of instant death or instant permanent impairing of any organ of the body or instant fear of being subjected to sodomy or *zina-bil-jabr*;

2. *"ikrah-e-naqis"* (إکراہ ناقص) means any form of duress which does not amount to *ikrah-i-tam*;

13.3 Mistake

Mistake is either mistake of law or mistake of fact. The general rule is that "ignorance of law is no excuse even in a layman." We will first deal with mistake of fact and then with mistake of law followed by the concept of mistake in Islamic law.

13.3.1 Mistake or Ignorance of fact

§79 of the PPC deals with mistake of fact in its usuall meaning, while §76 deals with mistake in the case of "superior orders." The reason is that §76 talks about persons believing themselves "bound by law" to perform their duty in a certain way, while §79 talks about the acts of the person who believes himself to be justified by law to act in the way he did. §79 states that:

> Nothing is an offence which is done by a person who is justified by law, or who by reason of a mistake of

> fact and not by reason of mistake of law in good faith, believes himself to be justified by law, in doing it.

The rules regarding mistake of fact may be summarized as follows:

1. **Mistake Must Negate State of Mind.** Ignorance or mistake as to a matter of fact will affect criminal guilt only if it is shown that the defendant did not have the state of mind required for the crime.

    > (1) A, hunting in the woods, shoots at what he reasonably believes to be a deer. In fact, it is Z, who is killed. A's mistake of fact establishes that he did not have the state of mind required for *qatl 'amd.* Under §318, he is guilty of *qatl khaṭa'* and not *qatl 'amd.* This is the result of a lawful act. What is the distinction between this and an accident as defined in the PPC? (examine the illustration to that section).
    >
    > (2) A, hunting in the woods, shoots through the trees at a figure he believes to be his enemy B, intending to kill him. In fact, the figure is C, who is killed. This is a case of transferred malice, because A's mistake does not negate his intent to kill a person. Is A guilty of *qatl 'amd?* Focus on the words "such person" in §300. Is he guilty of *shibh al-'amd?*

2. **The Mistake Should be Reasonable.** The mistake or ignorance should be one that is expected of a reasonable man. This, however, is said to apply to crimes that require a general intent. In the case of sepcific intent crimes, any mistake, reasonable or unreasonable, is a defence.

    > A, leaving a restaurant, takes an umbrella, believing that it was the one he had left there a week ago. In fact, it belongs to B. Is A guilty of theft? Here A lacked a specific intent to deprive B of his property. Since his mistake negates a specific intent, it is not material whether it was a reasonable mistake or not.

3. **Mistake is no Defence in Strict Liability Crimes.** Since strict liability crimes require no state of mind, mistake or ignorance of fact is, therefore, no defence to them.

13.3.2 Mistake or Ignorance of Law

As a general rule, it is not a defence to a crime that the defendant was unaware that his acts were prohibited by the criminal law or that he mistakenly believed that his acts were not prohibited. This is true even if his ignorance or mistake was reasonable. In the present age, Courts all over the world are prepared to acknowledge some exceptions:

1. **Statute not reasonably available.** The defendant has a defence if the statute proscribing his conduct was not published or made reasonably available prior to the conduct.

2. **Reasonable reliance upon statute or judicial decision.** The defendant has a defence if he acted in reasonable reliance upon a statute or judicial decision, even though the statute is later declared unconstitutional or the decision is overruled.

3. **Reasonable reliance upon official interpretation or advice.** At common law, it was not defence that the defendant relied upon an erroneous official statement of the law contained in an administrative order or grant or in an official interpretation by the public officer or body responsible for interpretation, administration, or enforcement of the law. In the United Stated, a new rule, advocated by the Model Penal Code provides a defence when the statement is obtained from one "charged by law with responsibility for the interpretation, administration, or enforcement of the law." As compared to this reliance upon advice of a lawyer is no defence.

13.3.3 Mistake in Islamic law—*jahl, shubhāt*

The word *shubhah* in its literal meaning is translated as "doubt," but that is not its technical meaning, at least in the context of the *ḥudūd.* The technical or legal translation of this terms should be "mistake."[170] The other words used in Islamic law are *jahl* (igno-

170. In contracts, some writers try to import the word *ghalaṭ* to identify the concept of mistakes in that law. It should be noted that *ghalaṭ* is

rance, uncertainty) and *khaṭa'* (mistake). All three are interrelated and deal with concepts that are similar to what in Western law are called mistake of law and mistake of fact.

For the word *shubhah* the most important evidence is the tradition of the Prophet (p.b.u.h.) in which it has been said that the *ḥudūd* penalties are to be waived in case of *shubhah.* As already indicated, this is usually taken to mean "benefit of doubt" given to the accused. While this meaning may be covered by the tradition it is not its primary concern. The rule of giving benefit of doubt to the accused is generally accepted as a rule of evidence in Islamic law. Further, this rule deals with the doubt in the mind of the judge as to whether an offence has been proved beyond doubt. The tradition, according to the jurists, deals with doubts in the mind of the offender at the time of commission or omission of an act. These are of several types:

1. Mistake of law:
   a) *shubhah fī al-dalīl* (mistake of law);
   b) *shubhah fī al-'aqd* (mistake as to the governing law in the contract);
2. Mistake of fact:
   a) *shubah fī al-milk* (mistake as to ownership); and
   b) *shubhah fī al-fi'l* (mistake in the commission of the act).

> Assume that in the early days there was a person who was under the impression that temporary marriage is permitted, that is, he may not be aware of the abrogating evidence. If he entered into a temporary marriage under this impression, the marriage contract was declared void, but the law would waive the *ḥadd* penalty in such a case (this does not mean that *ta'zīr* was also waived). There could have been a possibility of the occurrence of such a case in the early days when people were not aware of the law. Today it is unlikely

a term used in the Egyptian law, relying on French law, and not in Islamic law.

> to happen. In any case, it is an example of *shubhah fī al-dalīl* as well as *shubhah fī al-'aqd.*
>
> If some of the heirs pardon the murderer, but some of the other heirs, who have not pardoned him, execute him, they will not be subjected to retaliation due to *shubhah fī al-dalīl* (mistake of law). They may be awarded *ta'zīr*. Today, these heirs are not permitted to take the law into their own hands.
>
> It should be obvious that exemptions for mistakes of law are given where the issue is subject to *ijtihād*. Where the matter is not subject to *ijtihād*, and is clearly known, or is supposed to be known to Muslims by necessity, there can be no exemption.
>
> In the early days, when slavery was permitted, a husband may be under the impression that his wife's slave girl is also within his ownership. Under this wrong impression if he were to consider her *milk yamīn* and act upon this belief he would be under *shubhah fī al-milk*. The *ḥadd* penalty would be waived in such a case (though not *ta'zīr*).
>
> If a man aiming at an animal were to hit a human being, he would be guilty of manslaughter (*qatl khaṭa'*) and not murder. This is an example of *shubhah fī al-fi'l.*

The law, gives, some exemption in such cases and lays down principles that may be applied to new cases. It can be seen with ease, however, that ignorance or mistake does not affect legal capacity in any way. The only problem here is that the understanding of the subject is hampered somewhat, but the law takes notice even of this. This shows that ignorance and mistake are not causes of defective capacity at all, but statutory grounds of defence or exemptions.

Jahl (ignorance) may, thus, be that of law or of fact. In general, ignorance of law is no excuse for a subject present within the *dār al-Islām*. This, however, should not be confused with the acts of a Muslim residing in the *dār al-ḥarb*. The Ḥanafīs make an exemption for some of the unlawful acts of such an individual, because he is not enjoying the protection of the Islamic state during his stay abroad. Submission to the Islamic state and being subject to its jurisdiction is also stated as a condition of *taklīf* by some jurists. The issue of jurisdiction of the Muslim state is expressed as a principle by the Ḥanafī jurist al-Dabūsī:

> The principle according to our jurists is that the world is divided into two *dārs*: *dār al-Islām* and *dār al-ḥarb*. According to Imām al-Shāfi'ī the entire world is a single *dār*.[171]

In other words, al-Shāfi'ī does not grant the same exemptions to an individual residing in enemy territory.

13.4 Consent

§§87 to 93 of the Pakistan Penal Code deal with consent as well as implied consent. Some of the situations described in these sections are obvious like sports, doctor-patient relationship, or things done for the benefit of a child or another person in good faith. Here we shall focus on the points that are related to crimes proper.

Consent of the victim is generally no defence. However, if it negates an element of the offence, consent is a complete defence.

> (a) Showing that the victim consented to intercourse is a defence to a charge of forcible rape.
>
> (b) Showing that an adult person consented to traveling with the defendant is a defence to kidnapping.

For some crimes, the consent of the victim is of no relevance, like raping a minor girl. For other offences, consent may be of limited effect (e.g., within limits, victim may consent to infliction of physical violence, and one inflicting it will therefore not be guilty of inflicting hurt).

Whenever consent may be a defence, it must be established that:

1. The consent was voluntarily and freely given (without compulsion or duress);
2. The party was legally capable of consenting; and
3. No fraud was involved in obtaining the consent.

171. Al-Dabūsī, *Ta'sīs al-Naẓar* (Cairo, 1320/1902), 58.

Forgiveness by the injured party after the crime has been committed ordinarily does not operate as a defence to the commission of a crime, unless a statute establishes such a defence. For example, *ḥadd* will not be enforced for theft liable to *ḥadd* "when, before the execution of *hadd*, the victim withdraws his allegation of theft."

13.4.1 Euthanasia and Islamic law

One of the major issues today is that of euthanasia and medically assisted suicide. It would be pertinent to record some of the views found in Islamic law on homicide with consent.

The Ḥanafīs, except Zufar, maintain that consent in the case of homicide, converts the offence *qatl 'amd* to *shibh al-'amd.* Thus, it acts as a mitigating factor. The reason is *shubhah* and *ḥadd, qiṣāṣ* being within its meaning, is to be waived when the victim has consented to his death. Zufar disagrees and says that consent does not amount to *shubhah.*[172]

The Mālikī jurists maintain that there is no *shubhah* in such a case and *qiṣāṣ* will be imposed.

The prominent opinion in the Shāfi'ī and Ḥanbalī schools is that neither *qiṣāṣ* nor *diyah* is imposed in such a case. The killing of the individual with consent becomes lawful, as it is the victim who has the right here, which he can lawfully exercise. It is just like the destruction of his own property.[173] This opinion, it appears, would consider euthanasia and medically assisted suicide as lawful.

13.5 The Right of Private Defence

The Pakistan Penal Code lays down the law on the right of private defence in §§96 to 106. §96 says that "[n]othing is an offence which is done in the exercise of the right of private defence." §97 divides it into the following types:

172. Al-Kāsānī, *Badā'i' al-Ṣanā'i'*, vol. 7, 236; Ibn 'Ābidīn, *al-Durr al-Mukhtār,* vol. 5, 388.
173. *Mughnī al-Muḥtāj,* vol. 4, 11; *Kashshāf al-Qinā'*, vol. 5, 206.

1. Defence of one's own body against any offence affecting the human body.
2. Defence of another person's body against any offence affecting the human body.
3. Defence of one's property, movable or immovable, against the offences of theft, robbery, mischief or criminal trespass.
4. Defence of another person's property, movable or immovable, against the offences of theft, robbery, mischief or criminal trespass.

The act may be exercised against a person of unsound mind, minor, intoxicated person or one under some misconception (§98). It cannot be exercised against a public servant acting in good faith or one acting on the directions of a public servant, unless there is apprehension of death or grievous hurt (§99). The right may be exercised even it amounts to hurting an innocent person alongwith the offender (§106).

13.5.1 How is the right exercised

The right of private defence may be exercised in the following ways:

1. **By use of deadly force that may lead to death:** This is divided into two categories depending on the type of right exercised.
    a) **Defending one's own body or that of another:** §100 lists the cases in which death may be caused. These are:
        i. apprehension of death as a result of the assault;
        ii. assault is with the intent to commit rape;
        iii. assault is with the intent to gratify unnatural lust;
        iv. assault is with the intention of kidnapping and abduction

b) **Defending one's property or the property of another:** §103 lists the cases as follows:

   i. threat of robbery;
   ii. threat of house-breaking by night;
   iii. mischief by fire commited on any building, tent or vessel when these are used as human dwellings or used for custody of property.
   iv. theft, mischief or house-trespass when there is apprehension that these will lead to death or grievous hurt.

2. **By use of non-deadly force that may cause harm other than death:** §§101 and 104 elaborate that when the threatened offences are not those mentioned above, the defender may use non-deadly force.

13.5.2 Private-defence and Islamic law

The right of private-defence in Islamic law is generally studied under the heading of *daf' al-ṣā'il* or warding off an assailant. The evidence for its legality is considered to be the verse of the Qur'ān that permits the use of aggression (*i'tidā'*) to ward of agression, but with similar force. The *sunnah* of the Prophet (p.b.u.h.) deems a person who dies defending his life, family or property a *shahīd*. Further, it asks the believer to help his believing brother who is defending himself, his family or his property.

The Ḥanafīs stipulate that the act of agression should be an offence. Thus, the right cannot be exercised against authority exercised in a lawful manner. The right, however, is available against a person who is himself in a state of *iṭirār* or necessity and is stealing to save his life.

The jurists also agree that a person who kills another in the exercise of the right of private-defence is not liable for *qiṣāṣ* or *diyah.* From this, the Ḥanafīs exempt the case of the minor, insane person and an animal. Liability in such cases is restricted to compensation and there is no criminal liability. The majority of the jurists maintain that there is no liability, criminal or financial, even in these cases. The Ḥanbalīs make a distinction and maintain that when a person is defending his own body, family or property, there is no liability, but when it is the body, family, or property of another there is financial liability.

Discussion Questions

1. Discuss the law pertaining to mistake under the Pakistan Penal Code, with special reference to mistake and "superior orders."
2. Is the law of mistake recognized by Islamic law? If so, in what form?
3. Distinguish between necessity and duress under the Penal Code and under Islamic law.
4. When is consent a defence under the Pakistan Penal Code?
5. Does Islamic law permit medically assisted suicide?
6. Elaborate the law of private defence as it is laid down in the Pakistan Penal Code. Under what situations can death be caused in the exercise of this right?
7. What problems can you point out, if any, in the exercise of the right of private defence under Islamic law?

CHAPTER 14

MENTAL CAPACITY DEFENCES

> *Crimes were committed to punish crimes, and crimes were committed to prevent crimes. The world has been filled with prisons and dungeons, with chains and whips, with crosses and gibbets, with thumbscrews and racks, with hangmen and heads-men—and yet these frightful means and instrumentalities have committed far more crimes than they have prevented.... Ignorance, filth, and poverty are the missionaries of crime. As long as dishonorable success outranks honest effort—as long as society bows and cringes before the great thieves, there will be little ones enough to fill the jails.*
>
> Robert Ingersoll,
> *Crimes Against Criminals*

14.1 Insanity as a Mental Capacity Defence

See the rules for insanity in the previous chapter.

14.2 Automatism as a Mental Capacity Defence

See the discussion for insanity in the previous chapter.

14.3 Intoxication

The principles governing intoxication by alcohol and by drugs are the same. Intoxication has never been a defence as such. Intoxication may be caused by any substance. Alcohol, drugs, and medicine are the most frequent. Evidence of intoxication may be raised whenever intoxication negates the existence of an element of a crime. The law generally distinguishes between voluntary and involuntary intoxication.

14.3.1 Voluntary intoxication

Intoxication is voluntary (self-induced) if it is the result of the intentional taking without duress of a substance known to be intoxicating. The person need not have intended to become intoxicated. In common law countries, where the use of alcohol is legal, voluntary intoxication is not, and has never been, in itself a defence.[174] In fact, in some offences, such as driving, or being in charge of a motor vehicle, under the influence of drink or drugs, or being disorderly in a public place, intoxication is the essence of the offence.[175] Here, however, we are concerned with intoxication as a defence. Though not a defence, voluntary intoxication is a factor relevant to criminal liability in three cases:

1. If a specific intent is an essential element of the offence charged and the accused's intoxication affords evidence that he lacked this intent. This is particularly true in cases of violence. Thus, if in his drunkenness the defendant was unable to appreciate that firing a gun at another was likely to harm him, the defendant has to introduce evidence to support his claim of lack of *mens rea*. This rule of specfic intent was settled in *DPP v Majewski*.[176] §86 of the PPC goes against this rule and maintains that voluntary intoxication cannot help in negating intent, even in specific intent cases (see section below).

2. Where a statute specifically provides that a particular belief shall be a defence to the offence charged. In England, §5 of the Criminal Damage Act, 1971 makes such a provision.

174. Cross and Jones, *Introduction to Criminal Law*, 109.
175. Ibid.
176. [1977] AC 443, [1976] All ER 142, HL.

3. If it causes such a disease of the mind as to bring the M'aghten Rules into play. Intoxication and insanity are two separate defences. However, continuous, excessive drinking or drug use may bring on actual insanity (e.g., *delirium tremens*). Thus, a defendant may be able to claim both an intoxication defence and an insanity defence.

14.3.2 Involuntary intoxication

Intoxication is involuntary only if it results from the taking of an intoxicating substance

1. without knowledge of its nature,
2. under direct duress imposed by another, or
3. pursuant to medical advice while unaware of the substance's intoxicating effect.

Involuntary intoxication may be treated as mental illness, in which case a defendant is entitled to acquittal if, because of the intoxication, he meets whatever test has been adopted for insanity. These tests are laid down in §§85 and 86 of the PPC. §85 states as follows:

> Nothing is an offence which is done by a person who, at the time of doing it, is, by reason of intoxication, incapable of knowing the nature of the act, or that he is doing what is either wrong, or contrary to law: **provided that the thing which intoxicated him was administered to him without his knowledge or against his will.**

§86 states that:

> In cases where an act done is not an offence unless done with a particular knowledge or intent, a person who does the act in a state of intoxication shall be liable to be dealt with as if he had the same knowledge as he would have had if he had not been intoxicated, **unless**

the thing which intoxicated him was administered to him without his knowledge or against his will.

§86 thus deals with offences of specific intent and elaborates that voluntary intoxication will have no effect on *mens rea.*

14.3.3 Intoxication and Islamic law

Intoxication (*sukr*) does not cause a change in the capacity for acquisition, as its basis is the attribute of being a human.[177] Thus, a drunken person possesses a *dhimmah* with a complete capacity for acquisition, and he is held liable for destruction of life and property, and also for all obligations, for maintenance, and even for *zakāt*. All these duties and obligations require the existence of the capacity for acquisition alone, and intoxication does not negate it.

The basis for the capacity for execution, on the other hand, is *'aql* and discretion; these are negated in the case of the drunken person by the state of drunkenness. The *khiṭāb*, it is maintained by some, is not addressed to the drunken person, because he does not comprehend it. The state of such a person is worse than that of one who is asleep, for the latter can be awakened; it is worse than that of an idiot, who may understand parts of the speech addressed to him.

The jurists agree unanimously that the *khiṭāb* is not directed toward the intoxicated person if such intoxication has been caused by the legal use of intoxicants. For example, the person who has consumed liquor without knowing what it is or when he has done so under coercion or under duress to save his life. In such cases, the *ḥukm* for this person will be the same as that of the person under a spell of fainting.

Muslim jurists disagree about the person who is intoxicated when such intoxication is caused by prohibited means, ie, in the case of voluntary intoxication. The Ḥanafīs and some other jurists do not consider such a cause to have any effect on the capacity for execution and on the understanding of the *khiṭāb*. Thus, the *'ibādāt* are established against such a person and he will be

177. Ṣadr al-Sharī'ah, *al-Tawḍīḥ*, vol. 2, 798.

held liable for delayed performance (*qaḍā'*), along with the accompanying sin. Any transaction or acknowledgement he makes is valid and enforceable against him. He acquires criminal liability for acts committed in such a state, though he can retract his confession made in this state regarding a case of *ḥudūd,* as these are pure rights of Allāh. The argument provided by the Ḥanafīs is that intoxication is a crime and as such cannot be an excuse for waiving punishments. Further, one reason why intoxication has been prohibited is that it leads to other *khabā'ith.* Moreover, if the acts of the drunken person are to be exempted from liability, it will become a means for the commission of offences, and for evading liability. Relying on the verse, "O ye believers, approach not prayer when you are intoxicated, until you know what you say," [Qur'ān 4 : 43] they maintain that it is obvious that the *khiṭāb* is addressed to the drunken person and he is expected to understand the meaning and import of the verse even when he is intoxicated. If this is not the interpretation, it would amount to saying to a person under a spell of madness, "Do not commit such an act when you are insane." It is for this reason that the drunken person is held liable for his acts.

Some jurists are of the opinion that an intoxicated person has no capacity for execution, because his *'aql* is completely impaired by the state of intoxication. They maintain that the Lawgiver has already provided a penalty for the offence of intoxication and holding him liable for his transactions as well, that is, those undertaken in such a state, would amount to punishing him twice for the same offence, a kind of double jeopardy. They argue that the verse about avoiding prayers in an intoxicated state is actually addressed to a sober person telling him to avoid becoming intoxicated before the time of prayer, an act over which he has control, as compared to the person subject to fits of madness over which he has no control.

Modern jurists try to prefer the second opinion as it may be closer to some forms of Western law, like the three cases mentioned above for voluntary intoxication. It must be noted, however, that consuming liquor is an offence in Islamic law and it may not be so in the law.

Discussion Questions

1. Distinguish between voluntary and involuntary intoxication and the defences available under each.
2. How does Islamic law view the defence of intoxication?

CHAPTER 15

OVERVIEW OF OFFENCES AND PENALTIES IN ISLAMIC LAW

Every society gets the kind of criminal it deserves. What is also true is that every community gets the kind of law enforcement it insists on.

John F. Kennedy (1917-1963)
Thirty-fifth President of the USA

The offences for which specified penalties are provided are called *ḥudūd.* Those in which *qiṣāṣ* or reparation is provided are called *jināyāt.* Punishments that are at the discretion of the judge when the offence is related to a private injury are called *ta'zīr.* Offences that are mainly directed against the system and society or where the pure right of the state is affected are called *siyāsah* penalties. Some offences that are corrected by acts of personal penance are called *kaffārāt* (expiation).

15.1 *Ḥadd* Penalties

Ḥadd is defined as penalty prescribed in the Qur'ān and the *Sunnah* as a pure right of Allah. Some jurists list seven such offences: *zinā* (unlawful sexual intercourse); *sariqah* (theft from a place of safe custody); *ḥirābah* (robbery with the force of arms); *qadhf* (false accusation of unlawful sexual intercourse); *shurb* (drinking of intoxicating beverages); *riddah* (apostasy); and *baghy* (rebellion). The last two are omitted by some jurists, who presumably consider apostasy and rebellion to fall under the *siyāsah* jurisdiction of the state. We shall describe the first five.

15.1.1 *Zinā* or unlawful sexual intercourse

Unlawful sexual intercourse is considered an offence against the right of Allah. It should not be confused with adultery, which is a Western concept. This offence consists in having sexual intercourse with any person not one's lawful spouse. In the case of males, Islamic law permits sexual intercourse in the case of *milk yamīn*, i.e., lawfully owned slave girls. It is for this reason that the Ḥanafīs define the offence as: "intercourse without *milk* or *shubhat milk*." *Milk* arises from a valid marriage or, in the case of males, ownership of a female slave. The *shubhat milk* is a mistake of fact of ownership and arises from an irregular marriage, marriage during *'iddah*, or in the case of an *umm al-walad* already set free or a slave girl sold but not delivered to the buyer or the slave girl of one's son or other near relative. In the cases of *shubhah*, the penalty of *ḥadd* is waived and may be replaced with *ta'zīr*.

The punishment for *zinā* in the case of a *muḥṣan* (married or once married) is *rajm* or death by stoning, with the Ẓāhirī school maintaining that 100 stripes are to be awarded before stoning. The Khārijīs denied the validity of *rajm* as the penalty is not mentioned in the Qur'ān. The punishment for the non-*muḥṣan* (never married) is 100 stripes, while exile or imprisonment for a year may be awarded as *ta'zīr*. The majority of the schools hold exile of one year to be part of the *ḥadd*.

The offence is proved through the testimony of four eligible witnesses who give evidence of the actual act of penetration. In the alternate, the accused must confess four times. The offence cannot be proved by circumstantial evidence, like pregnancy, except in the opinion of Mālik. The action against the perpetrator, especially according to the Ḥanafīs, should not be delayed. Many jurists believe that it is recommended and meritorious for the witnesses or complainants to refrain from bringing charges against the perpetrator so as to protect society from the consequences of publicity and to enable the person to settle the offence privately with Allah. The *Hidāyah*, for example, begins the description of the offence with this recommendation. If this is the recommendation for *ḥadd*, then, it may be argued that *ta'zīr* for such offences is not justified; there should only be the offence of *ḥadd* along with its conditions of proof. Of course, rape is a different matter.

15.1.2 *Qadhf* or false accusation of unlawful sexual intercourse

The meaning of the word *muḥṣan* is different for the offence of *qadhf* and here it means one who is chaste, i.e., he or she has not been convicted for the offence of *zinā;* being married is not a condition. Anyone who is competent and adult, whether male or a female, Muslim or not, slave or free is liable if he falsely charges a chaste person (*muḥṣan*) with unlawful sexual intercourse (*zinā*) or charges one of being illegitimate. Thus, the offence can be committed by making such an accusation against a dead person and in this case the aggrieved persons would be the children.

The punishment of *qadhf* is 80 stripes for a free person and forty for a slave. The offence is proved by confession or testimony of two adult male free Muslims. The defence is possible by producing 4 witnesses who shall testify to *zinā* committed by the complainant or the person accused of *zinā.*

A husband who makes a charge against his wife is also liable to *hadd,* unless he adopts the procedure of *li'ān.* This involves a charge of *zinā* or denial of the paternity of the child by swearing four times by Allah that he is speaking the truth and a fifth time he calls down a curse upon himself if he is lying. The wife can deny such a charge in a similar fashion and her word is given preference.

15.1.3 *Shurb* or drinking of wine or intoxicating beverages

There are two separate offences under this head according to the Ḥanafīs: drinking *khamr* (wine) in any quantity, and being intoxicated by another prohibited beverage. As to what is a prohibited beverage is a matter of dispute among the Ḥanafī jurists. The other schools do not make any distinction between the beverages and each intoxicating liquor is designated as *khamr* the consumption of which is punishable whatever the quantity consumed. Actual intoxication thus is not a separate crime according to these schools. The Prohibition Order has preferred the majority opinion and not the Ḥanafī view. There is, thus, a single offence liable to *ḥadd* under the Order.

The crime is proved by the testimony of two adult male witnesses who should see the accused drinking and should testify while the smell of the drink is on the person of the accused, unless delay is caused due to unavoidable circumstances. This is the view of the Ḥanafīs except, Muḥammad al-Shaybānī. The other jurists, especially Mālik, allow proof of the offence by intoxication as well as smell.

15.1.4 *Sariqah* or theft

The offence of *sariqah* or theft is committed if the offender takes from a place of safe custody (*ḥirz*) by stealth property of the value of one dinar according to the Ḥanafīs and 1/4 dinar according to the majority in which he has neither the right of ownership (*milk*) or semblance of ownership (*shubhat milk*). A basic ingredient of this offence, according to all the schools, is that the property stolen must be owned by someone. The Theft Ordinance implemented in Pakistan drops this condition, apparently to accommodate ownership of juristic persons as the concept of juristic person is not recognized by Islamic law. *Ḥirz* is of two kinds: by itself (*bi'l-makān*) and by a guard or watchman (*bi'l-ḥifẓ*).

The charge must be brought by the owner unless of course the thief himself confesses. If the thief repents and returns the property he cannot be accused. The offence is proved by the testimony of two persons who should see the thief removing the property from the *ḥirz*. Some jurists do not impose the condition of *ḥirz* nor of the *niṣāb*, i.e., the minimum value of one dinar, the Ẓāhirīs being the foremost among them. The condition of *shubhat milk* removes from the ambit of the offence a large number of cases. *Ta'zīr*, however, can be implemented in these cases and in cases where other conditions of proof for *ḥadd* are not met.

15.1.5 *Ḥirābah* or Highway Robbery

This offence is also referred to as major (*kubrā*) theft and the previous one as minor (*sughrā*) theft. The crime is also related to the offence of homicide. It is a serious offence having different penalties varying with the nature of the case. It may first be divided into robbery of travellers who are far from aid, and armed entrance into a private home with an intent to rob it. Punishments range from amputation of the right hand and left foot for the first offence and amputation of the left hand and right foot for the second offence. The condition of the *nisāb* is also imposed after dividing the property taken amongst the culprits. If only death has been caused. punishment is death by the sword as *ḥadd* and not as *qiṣāṣ*. Homicide along with plunder invoke the punishment of crucifixion. Each person involved in the crime is liable for the punishment whatever the nature of his individual act. However, if one is a minor *ḥadd* lapses for the others as well. If the offender repents and surrenders before apprehension, the *ḥadd* is waived, but any liability for homicide in such a case is subjected to *qiṣāṣ* proceedings for settlement.

15.1.6 Apostasy (*Riddah*)

Apostasy or *riddah* invokes the penalty of death for men. Apostasy occurs when the offender rejects Islam by commission or omission with the awareness of the penalty. From some texts of the jurists it appears that crossing over to the *dār al-ḥarb*, i.e., joining the enemy may be essential for the completion of this crime. This, however, is not the general view. Some time is given to the accused to repent which ranges from three days to the discretion of the state. The penalty of death being for men, women are to be subjected to physical punishment with an interval of three days till they repent. Rebellion (*baghy*) is also considered by some as *ḥadd*.

15.2 *Jināyat* (Bodily Injuries) and *Qiṣāṣ*

The word *jināyah,* as explained above, means damage to property as well as homicide and bodily harm. In pre-Islamic times an attack against a tribesman was treated as an attack against the tribe itself. Retaliation was against the tribe of the offender though sometimes the actual offender could be punished through arbitration. Islamic law modified the traditional Arab law in three ways:

1. The blood feud was abolished.
2. Vengeance could be exacted only after determining guilt of the accused through judicial proceedings. The crimes were to be proved by two witnesses or by confession. Where the killer is not known the method of compurgation *qasāmah* is adopted for differing purposes according to the different schools.
3. Different punishments were laid down for different offences according to the degree of culpability.

In the case of homicide, four kinds of punishments have been laid down by the *sharī'a*: *qiṣāṣ* (retaliation), *diyah* (blood money), *kaffārah* (expiation), and prevention from inheritance whenever relevant. The kinds of acts leading to death of the victim are divided in different ways by the jurists. The division preferred by the majority of the Ḥanafīs is as follows:

15.2.1 *Qatl 'Amd* or Murder

This is the case of deliberate intent which implies the use of a deadly weapon which is meant to cause death. The weapon must be one that is usually "prepared for killing." Modern day guns and knives would therefore be included. The standard used for determining culpability for this offence is external. It is only the Mālikī jurists who do not judge the offence by the use of a weapon and mere hostility of the offender towards the victim is considered sufficient. The offence entails *qiṣaṣ* (retaliation) and there is no *kaffārah* (expiation) in it according to the Ḥanafīs. Retaliation, however, can be waived by way of pardon (*'afw*) gratis or by charging a sum of money, which may be more or less than the *diyah*, by way of *sulh* (settlement) or by claiming the *diyah*. The Ḥanafīs do not allow the claiming of the *diyah* without the consent of the offender. The killer cannot inherit from the deceased.

15.2.2 *Shibh al-'amd* or culpable homicide not amounting to murder

The Mālikīs do not recognize this kind of offence and merge it with the first one. According to the majority, the offence is committed if the weapon used is not "readied for killing." The Ḥanafīs maintain that killing with a blunt weapon will result in this offence and not murder. The exception is killing with an iron rod, because the Qur'ān says that there is great strength in iron. The majority are somewhat lenient on this count. In Mālikī law a person can be guilty, as has been noted above, only of with the intent to cause harm, i.e., through *'udwān* or an act of hostility . As both offences combined amount to murder under the Mālikī system, their definition of murder is very wide.

The new provisions of the PPC pertaining to *qiṣāṣ* and *diyah* mix the eternal standards used by the Ḥanafīs as well as the subjective standards of the common law that attempt to discover what "went on in the mind of the accused." This may result in confusion in applying the law.

The penalty for *shibh al-'amd* is "enhanced" blood money to be paid by the *'āqilah* along with expiation. The killer is also debarred from inheriting from the victim.

15.2.3 *Qatl khaṭa'* or manslaughter

This covers cases of mistake or *khaṭa'* and cases that run on the same lines as mistake. There are different types of such mistakes. They may be divided into two broad types on basis of whether the act is voluntary or involuntary:

1. *Voluntary acts:* This has further three types:

    a) The first may be called mistake of purpose, which arises, for example, when a person shoots and kills something which he believes to be an animal but which is in fact a human being.

    b) Another case is that of mistake in performance where a person aims at a target but misses and kills someone.

    c) In both the above cases the act is deliberate and intrinsically likely to kill but is not directed against a human being. If it were directed against a human being and someone other than the victim is killed, i.e., in case of transferred malice, it is only the Ḥanbalī law that considers it as *'amd.* The majority consider even this as manslaughter or *khaṭa'.*

2. *Involuntary act:* This is the case of *shibh al-khaṭa'* in which the act is wholly involuntary. This is the case, for example, if a person falls from a height upon another person and kills him or something slips from his hand and falls on another. A driver losing control of his vehicle and killing a pedestrian would be liable under this head.

Blood money is to be paid by the *'āqilah* in all cases of *khaṭa',* and the killer cannot inherit from the victim.

15.2.4 *Qatl bi-al-sabab* or indirect homicide

The majority, except for the Mālikīs, draw draw a distinction between a direct killing (*mubāsharatan*) and an indirect killing (*qatl bi-al-sabab*). Indirect homicide may be intentional or unintentional. Intentional homicide amounts to *qatl 'amd* and the offender is to be subjected to *qiṣāṣ.* The Ḥanafīs, however, maintain that *qiṣāṣ* means equality and to maintain equality retaliation should also be implemented indirectly. As this is not possible the penalty is converted to blood money to be paid by the offender himself and not by his *'āqilah.* The well known example of indirect homicide is killing by perjury.

Unintentional indirect killing leads to liability for blood money, however, the offender is not liable to *kaffārah* nor is he debarred from inheritance.

15.2.5 Justifiable homicide

Homicide which is not actionable is the execution of a death sentence, the killing of an outlaw as he is not legally protected, killing in self defence and sometimes in grave provocation. Death resulting from medical treatment with the consent of the deceased.

15.2.6 Bodily harm

There is no category of *shibh al-'amd* or quasi-*'amd* in cases of bodily harm other than homicide. Retaliation is possible where exact equality can be maintained and there is no danger of exceeding the extent of the injury caused. Accordingly, cutting of the bones from other than the joints is not permitted as exact equality cannot be maintained in such cases. Fractions of the *diyah* are fixed as compensation for different cases. For injuries to the skull the compensation is estimated and is called *ḥukūmah*.

15.3 *Ta'zīr* or penalties imposed by the state

The word *ta'zīr* is sometimes translated as discretionary penalties. This may be misleading insofar as discretionary means offences and penalties determined arbitrarily. This may be against the principle of legality. It really means those offences that may or may not be made culpable by the state. Today, the distinction between *ta'zīr* and *siyāsah* is not maintained so the bulk of the criminal offences in Islamic law are covered by *ta'zīr*.

It has been maintained that the distinction between *ḥadd* and *ta'zīr* punishments did not exist during the time of the Holy Prophet (p.b.u.h) but was devised later by the jurists in response to the needs of the early Islamic empire of the Umayyads. It is implied in the alternate that there were no *ta'zīr* punishments in the early days and *ta'zīr* grew later out of the discretionary punishments imposed by the *gāḍī*. The matter is of fundamental importance and concerns the doctrine of *ḥadd* itself. The Muslim jurists have, however, relied on some traditions to justify the existence of *ta'zīr* penalties even in the days of the Holy Prophet (p.b.u.h.).

The object of *ta'zīr* is reformation and the degree of punishment to cause this varies with each individual. Men are classified systematically by some jurists like al-Kāsāni into four classes: 1) the most distinguished of the upper classes; i.e. officials and officers of the highest rank (who usually belonged to the ruling family in those days); for them a communication from the judge through a confidential messenger is sufficient; 2) the notables, i.e. the intellectual elite and the *fuqahā'*; they are summoned by the *qāḍī* and admonished by him; the middle classes, i.e., the merchants: they are punished by imprisonment; 4) the lower strata of the people: they are punished with imprisonment of flogging. This type of classification, as is obvious, cannot be valid for the present times as it is against the principle of "rule of law," which requires that every person be treated equally.

The punishments cover a range of severity as follows:

a) a private admonition to the guilty party, sometimes by letter; b) a public reprimand in court; c) a public proclamation of the offenders guilt (tashhīr); d) a suspended sentence; e) banishment; f) a fine; 9) flogging (which may be inflicted with severity greater than that permitted for *ḥadd*); h) imprisonment; and i) death. If it seems advisable to the judge he can completely remit the *ta'zīr*, but a claim of the individual shall stand.

The process of trial is simple in contrast to that for *ḥadd*. *Ta'zīr* is inflicted on a confession even if withdrawn or on the testimony of two witnesses one of whom can be replaced by two women. Substituted testimony (*shahādah 'alā shahādah*) is also admitted. According to some, the judge can even render judgement on the basis of his own knowledge.

Offences under *ta'zīr* include perjury, usury, and slander. Many thefts, acts of unlawful intercourse, and false accusations of unlawful intercourse that escape the rigorous rules under the *ḥadd* punishments can be dealt with under *ta'zīr*. Offences under *ta'zīr* may, however, be divided into three broad classes. First. are the crimes which belong to the genus of the offences punishable under *ḥadd* and that fall short of the act that entails *ḥadd,* like preliminaries to unlawful intercourse or simple larceny and so on. Second, those crimes that are normally punishable under *ḥadd,* but in which by reason of mistake of law or fact or other reasons the penalty is replaced by *ta'zir.* Finally, those which are not punished by *ḥadd* but fall under the provisions of the law, i.e., an express justification in the text like: consumption of pork, breach of a trust by a guardian, false testimony, usury, slander and corruption generally.

The discretionary element of *ta'zīr* punishments has perhaps prevented the development of the subject by the Muslim jurists who have rarely dealt with it systematically. It is worth mentioning here that the penal programme of *ta'zīr* conceived by these jurists is no longer practicable today. The general principles, however, can be given effect in the form of individualization of punishment and reformation of the offender. With the codification of the law in the present times the discretion of the *qāḍī* shall be severely restricted within the scales of penalties provided for different offences. Further, a very flimsy barrier can be recognized or put up today between *ta'zīr* and *siyāsah* punishments.

15.4 *Siyāsah shar'īyah* or the administration of justice

The meaning of *siyāsah* has already been discussed above. According to this doctrine the Muslim ruler is granted a broad discretion to deal with the criminal offences, provided his acts do not blatantly violate the principles of *sharī'ah.* This is ensured when he seeks to protect and preserve the interests recognized by the *sharī'ah* in a manner described earlier. He, thus, possesses by virtue of this authority power to inflict severer punishments on a much wider scale than is available to the judge under *ḥudūd* and *ta'zīr.*

Western writers have tried to show that *siyāsah* punishments were purely a secular matter. Muslim jurists, on the other hand, like al-Māwardī al-Qarāfī, Ibn Taymīyah, Ibn al-Qayyim and Tarābalusī have all tried to show that not only is *siyāsah* compatible with the *sharī'ah* but envelopes the entire law though the term is usually applied to administrative penalties determined by the ruler. They also maintain that the basis of *siyāsah* is its concern with the public interest (*maṣlaḥah 'āmmah*), which varies with time and place. It is for this reason that *siyāsah* regulations must change and conform to the needs of the time. These regulations have been applied mostly by the *maẓālim* courts that enjoyed a much wider jurisdiction and great flexibility of procedure as compared to the court of the *qāḍī*

One of the essential conditions stipulated to ensure that *siyāsah* provisions laid down by the ruler shall conform to the principles of the *sharī'ah* is that the ruler must be a *mujtahid.* In practice, however, he seeks the approval of whosoever is the *mujtahid* of the age. At least, this is what the Ottoman Sultans practised when they issued their *qānūn'namas.* Approval was sought for all such provisions from the *shaykh al-Islām.* According to the codes of these rulers punishments by way of *siyasah* were to be inflicted for various crimes not covered by the strict *sharī'ah* law and for many other crimes which could not be proved by the strict procedure of the *qaḍī* courts. The punishments awarded during the times of the Turks were execution, amputation, stripes, exile, branding of the forehead, servitude on the galleys, shaving off of the beard, confiscation of property and fines. Most of these punishments were awarded according to the spirit of the times and cannot be considered as binding precedents.

In our own times a governmental decree issued in 1961 by the Government of Saudi Arabia allowed a *qāḍī* to go beyond the Ḥanbalī rules if the decision was faithful to the sources of the Islamic law. Under its *siyāsah* jurisdiction the government established boards to deal with matters relating to commerce, labour, taxation and traffic. Penalties have also been legislated under this jurisdiction. Higher courts have been established and *maẓālim* courts are also functioning.

15.5 *Ghaṣb* (Usurpation, Misappropriation)

The word *ghaṣb* (usurpation) and *itlāf* (destruction) are subtypes of the word *jināyah* (crime, tort), which is a term that includes both crimes and torts in their modern day meaning. *Itlāf* is treated as part of *ghaṣb* by some jurists, while others treat it separately.

The word *ghaṣb,* in its literal sense, means the taking by force of a thing from another for utilization. In its technical meaning it is defined as: "The taking of a protected marketable thing without the permission of the owner and in a manner that deprives the owner of its possession." The word "protected" means legally protected and thus excludes enemy property. The word "marketable" (*mutaqawwam*) means things that have no marketable value, like wine, swine and other non-marketable things. The stipulation of loss of possession is designed to exclude benefits or mesne profits and these cannot be the subject of *ghaṣb,* at least according to the Ḥanafīs. Here one should refer to the issue of damages, discussed earlier, where it was said that compensatory damages and wages or lost profits cannot be combined in one award. Further, according to the above meaning, the abduction of slaves would be included in the meaning of *ghaṣb,* but not the abduction of free persons.

There are three types of liability associated with *ghaṣb:*

1. Sin in the hereafter.
2. Restitution of property as long as it exists in its original form.
3. *Ḍamān* (compensatory damages) if the property is destroyed. Compensation for fungibles is through payment by *mithl* (similar) and where that is not possible payment is by *qīmah* (value).

There are detailed rules for things that have changed in shape, have grown or yielded mesne profits, while in the possession of the usurper.

15.6 Destruction of Property (*Itlāf*)

Destruction of property takes place either after *ghaṣb* or without it. Technically, it is defined as the conversion of property so that its usual intended benefits are no longer available to the owner. In fact, the offence is technically that of *ghaṣb,* because destruction of property in most cases may be treated as *ghaṣb* first and then *itlāf.*

The causing of miscarriage in the case of slave girls would fall under this head. Further, unlawful confinement of a person till such time that some of his property is wasted due to lack of care also invokes compensatory damages, besides the criminal liability. The usual liability in cases of destruction of property is compensatory damages.

Discussion Questions

1. The offence of *zinā bil-jabr* has recently been converted into the offence of rape in the PPC. The *fuqahā* always included it within the general offence of *zinā*. Can you argue in support of their classification of this offence?
2. Justify the exclusion of the *zinā bil-jabr* from the general offence of *zinā* and its classification as rape.
3. The offence of apostsy (*riddah*) is not treated as a *ḥadd* by most jurists. Do you think it is an offence that pertains to wartime and to joining the enemy against the Muslims?
4. The offence of *qadhf* ensures that the privacy of an individual is protected. Do you think that the sensational publication of news by the media should be subject to this offence?
5. What in your view is the philosophy underlying the offences classified as *jināyāt*? In other words, argue for the law of talion and regime of reparation associated with it.
6. Why in your view has the punishment of amputation of the hand has not been awarded during the years the Ordinance pertaining to *sariqah* has been in force?

BIBLIOGRAPHY

Nyazee, Imran Ahsan Khan. *Legal System of Pakistan*. Islamabad: Federal Law House, 2016.

Sarakhsī, Shams al-A'immah. *Kitāb al-Mabsūṭ*. Edited by Abū 'Abd Allāh Ismā'īl al Shāfi'ī. 30 vols. Beirut: Dār al-Kutub al-'Ilmiyyah, 2001.

Aarnio, Aulis. *Essays on the Doctrinal Study of Law*. London: Springer, 2011.

American Bar Association, Task Force on Law Schools and the Profession. *Legal Education and Professional Development: An Educational Continuum*. Chicago: American Bar Association, 1992.

Anne Colby, William Sullivan, and Judith Welch Wegner. *Educating Lawyers: Preparation for the Profession of Law*. San Francisco: The Carnegie Foundation for the Advancement of Teaching, 2007.

Austin, John. *The Province of Jurisprudence Determined*. London: John Murray, 1832.

Bentham, Jeremy. *An Introduction to the Principles of Morals and Legisltation*. 2nd ed. London: Clarendon Press, 1907.

Blackstone, William. *The Commentaries on the Laws of England*. 4 vols. London: John Murray, Albemarle Street, 1876.

Bodenheimer, Edgar. *Jurisprudence: The Philosophy and Method of the Law*. 2nd ed. Cambridge, Mass.: Harvard University Press, 1974.

Card, Richard. *Cross and Jones: Introduction to Criminal Law*. London: Butterworths, 1985.

Cross, Sir Rupert. *The English Sentencing System*. 3rd ed. London: Butterworths, 1981.

Dainow, Joseph. "The Civil Law and the Common Law: Some Points of Comparison." *American Society of Comparative Law* 15 (1967): 419–435.

Dressler, Joshua. *Understanding Criminal Law*. 2nd ed. New York: McGraw-Hill Higher Education, 1995.

Dworkin, Ronald. *Taking Rights Seriously*. Cambridge, Mass.: Harvard University Press, 1978.

Eisenberg, Melvin Aron. *The Nature of the Common Law*. Cambridge, MA: Harvard University Press, 1988.

Elliott, Catherine, and Frances Quinn. *Criminal Law*. 8th ed. Essex: Pearson Education Limited, 2010.

Farnsworth, E. Allan. *An Introduction to the Legal System of the United States*. Edited by Steve Sheppard. Oxford: Oxford University Press, 2010.

Galloway, Archibald. *Observations on the Law and Constitution of India: Landed Tenures and Financial Resources*. 2nd ed. London: Parbury, Allen & Co., 1832.

Geary, Roger. *Understanding Criminal Law*. London: Cavendish Publishing Limited, 2002.

Harris, Phil. *An Introduction to Law*. 7th ed. Cambridge: Cambridge University Press, 2007.

Hart, H. L. A. *The Concept of Law*. Oxford University Press, 1994.

Hertel, Christian. "Comparative Law: Legal Systems of the World—An Overview." *Notarius International* 2 (2009): 128–141.

Hohfeld, Wesley Newcomb. *Fundamental Legal Conceptions: As Applied in Judicial Reasoning*. New Haven: Yale University Press, 1920.

Holmes, Oliver Wendell. *The Common Law*. 2nd ed. Cambridge, Mass.: The Belknapp Press of Harvard University Press, 2009.

Kenny, Courtney Stanhope. *Outlines of Criminal Law*. 2nd ed. New York, NY: The Macmillan Company, 1907.

Llewellyn, Karl Nickerson. *The Common Law Tradition: Deciding Appeals*. 1st ed. Boston: Little, Brown & Co., 1960.

Macaulay, Thomas Babington. *Speeches and Poems With the Report and Notes on the Indian Penal Code*. Vol. 2. New York: Hurd & Houghton, 1867.

Omerod, David. *Criminal Law: Smith & Hogan*. 11th ed. Oxford: Oxford University Press, 2005.

Parisil, Francesco. "Rent-seeking Through Litigation: Adversarial and Inquisitorial Systems Compared." *International Review of Law and Economics* 22 (2002): 196–213.

Raz, Joseph. "The Identity of Legal Systems." *California Law Review* 59 (1971): 795–815.

Scheb, John M., and John M. Scheb II. *Criminal Law and Procedure*. 7th ed. Belmont, CA: Wadsworth, Cengage Learning, 2011.

Smith, J. C., and Brian Hogan. *Criminal Law*. 2nd ed. London: Butterworths, 1983.

Zander, Michael. *Cases and Materials on the English Legal System*. Cambridge: Cambridge University Press, 2007.

INDEX

abetment, 149, 153
  and innocent agent, 155
  and Islamic law, 158
  by aiding, 154
  by conspiracy, 154
  by instigation, 153
  through omission, 155
abettor, 149
  under the PPC, 155
accessories, 147
accomplice liability, 147
act and omission, 122
actus reus, 115
  circumstances, 115
  conduct, 115
  consequences, 115
actus reus
  and omission, 122
  concurrence with *mens rea*, 132
  involuntary, 121
  rules for, 117
  voluntary, 119
adversarial process, 103
aiding, 153
aims of criminal law, 69
'amd (intention), 133
  and external standards, 133
American Law Institute (ALI), 69
  insanity test, 169
analogy and criminal law, 50
apostasy, 199
attempt, 157
  and Islamic law, 158
automatism, 120

basic *mens rea*, 131
Bentham, Jeremy, 73
blasphemy, 143
bodily injuries, 200

Card, Richard, 9
classification of crimes, 53
  and rights, 57
  in Islamic law, 57
  modern, 67
coercion, 177
complicity, 147
concurrence of *mens rea* and *actus reus*, 132
consent, 184
conspiracy, 153
crime
  a moral wrong, 18
  a public wrong, 16
  and criminal proceedings, 20
  and offence, 22
  definition of, 15
crime creation, 49
  constitutional limitations, 49
crimes
  and morality, 18
  and strict liability, 141
  classification of, 53
  integrative approach to, 99
criminal law
  and *maqāṣid*, 70
criminal act, 115

as omission, 122
circumstances, 115
conduct, 115
consequences, 115
involuntary, 121
rules for, 117
voluntary, 119
criminal intent, 125
criminal law
aims of, 69
and interests, 71
and protection of interests, 71
sources for Pakistan, 29
criminal liability, 111
and general defences, 175
criminal proceedings
and crime, 20
criminal statutes
interpretation, 50
Cross, Rupert, 9

deterrence, 92
and *qiṣāṣ*, 95
and habitual offenders, 96
and Islamic law, 95
discretionary penalties, 203
doctrines of criminal law, 27
doubt, 182
drinking wine, 197
duress, 176, 177
and Islamic law, 177

education in criminal law, 26
elements of crime, 111
actus reus, 115
nature of, 112
enforcement of morality, 20
euthanasia
and Islamic law, 185

function of propositions, 27

general defences, 175
consent, 184
duress, 176
infancy, 161
insanity, 166
intoxication, 189
mistake, 179
necessity, 175
private-defence, 185
general intent, 127
general principles of Pakistani law, 26
ghaṣb, 207
guilt and retribution, 86

habitual offenders, 96
ḥadd and *ta'zīr*, 61
Hall, Jerome, 9, 27
ḥirābah, 198
Hogan, Brian, 9
ḥudūd, 16

ignorance, 182
of fact, 179
of law, 181
imprisonment
and Islamic law, 78
inchoate offences, 156
infancy, 161
and Islamic law, 162, 164
and the PPC, 162
presumption at common law, 161
innocent agent, 155
inquisitorial process, 103
insanity, 166
and Islamic law, 169
and the PPC, 166
criminal proceedings, 170
M'Naghten Rules, 167
instigation, 153
integrative approach, 99
intent

transferred, 128
intention, 125, 126
and motive, 128
direct, 126
oblique, 126
interpretation, 26
criminal statutes, 50
intoxicants, 197
intoxication, 189
and Islamic law, 192
involuntary, 191
voluntary, 190
involuntary act, 121
irresistable impulse, 168
Islamic law
and *mens rea*, 133
and abetment, 158
and attempt, 158
and deterrence, 95
and duress, 177
and euthanasia, 185
and imprisonment, 78
and infancy, 162, 164
and insanity, 169
and intoxication, 192
and legality, 47
and mistake, 181
and necessity, 176
and negligence, 138
and private-defence, 187
and retribution, 88
and strict liability, 145
comparison with, 9
Islamization of criminal law, 26
itlāf, 208

jarīmah, 23
jināyah, 23
jināyāt, 200
justifiable homicide, 203

legality, 45
and Islamic law, 47

liability of corporations, 172

malice
transferred, 128
manslaughter, 201
maqāṣid al-sharī'ah, 70
maṣlaḥah
and utility, 76
mens rea, 125
and Islamic law, 133
and negligence, 136
basic, 131
concurrence with *actus reus*, 132
meaning of, 125
misappropriation, 207
mistake, 179
and *shubhah*, 182
and Islamic law, 181
mistakes, 59
M'Naghten Rules, 167
Model Penal Code, 69, 73
modern classification of crimes, 67
morality
and crime, 18
and law, 83
motive, 128
murder, 200

nature of elements of crime, 112
necessity, 175
and Islamic law, 176
negligence, 131
and *mens rea*, 136
and Islamic law, 138
violation of objective standard, 136
nulla poena sine lege, 45

offence
and crime, 22
offences, 195

and strict liability, 141
classification of, 53
inchoate, 156
omission and act, 122

penalties, 195
perpetrator, 148
petty offences, 23
prevention, 98
primary deterrence, 92
principals, 147
principle of legality, 45
in Islam, 47
principles
meaning of, 29
principles of Western law, 26
private-defence, 185
and Islamic law, 187
propositions
function of, 27
propositions of criminal law, 27
protection of the public, 92
punishment, 73
and rights, 77
as deterrence, 92
as justice, 91
as retribution, 82
ingredients of, 73–75
nature of, 73
theories of, 81
types of, 77

qadhf, 197
qatl 'amd, 200
qatl bi al-sabab, 202
qatl khaṭa', 201
qiṣāṣ
meaning of, 88
qiyās and criminal law, 50

recklessness, 130
reformation, 97
rehabilitation, 97
retribution, 82
morality, 83
and guilt, 86
and Islamic law, 88
and vengeance, 89
as harm done, 90
as justice, 91
riddah, 199
rules of criminal law, 27

secondary deterrence, 92
sentencing, 73
shibh al-'amd, 201
shubhāt, 59, 182
shubhāt
and mistake, 182
siyāsah, 16, 205
siyāsah and *ta'zīr*, 64
Smith, J.C., 9
sources of criminal law, 29
specific intent, 127
strict liability
and Islamic law, 145
and vicarious liability, 172
at common law, 142
meaning of, 142
offences in Pakistan, 143
recognition of offences, 143
why imposed?, 144
strict liability offences, 141
structure of criminal law, 25, 27

ta'zīr, 16, 203
ta'zīr and *ḥadd*, 61
ta'zīr and *siyāsah*, 64
theories of punishment, 81
theory of retribution, 82
transferred intent, 128
transition to Islamic principles, 26

usurpation, 207
utility

and *maṣlaḥah*, 76
principle of, 76

vengeance, 89
vicarious liability, 171
and corporations, 172
and strict liability, 172
void-for-vagueness rule, 49
voluntary act, 119

zinā, 195

About This Book

This book compares the general principles of Western criminal law with those of Islamic law. Experience indicates that some people are irritated, or find it difficult to concentrate, when the text stands completely merged during comparison of two legal systems. This book, therefore, adopts a different methodology. Under each main heading in a chapter, it presents the Western point of view first. Once this has been explained, the Islamic point of view on the same issue is stated whenever it is felt necessary or is available. This method will not only assist the reader in understanding better the two points of view, but will also help those who wish to skip either point of view. On certain occasions a complete merger is unavoidable.

It should be noted that this is a preliminary book and it will not be possible to state the position of Islamic law on each point or in such detail that may be expected. This does not mean that there are no views from the perspective of Islamic law on the issue; it means that a fuller comparison can only be undertaken in a more comprehensive study.

www.ingramcontent.com/pod-product-compliance
Lightning Source LLC
Chambersburg PA
CBHW071421180526
45170CB00001B/174
9781541167148